FUNCTIONAL ARCHITECTURE

THE INTERNATIONAL STYLE

FUNKTIONALE ARCHITEKTUR

LE STYLE INTERNATIONAL

1925 – 1940

FUNCTIONAL ARCHITECTURE

BENEDIKT TASCHEN

© 1990 Benedikt Taschen Verlag GmbH & Co. KG
Hohenzollernring 53, D-5000 Köln 1
Printed in Germany
ISBN 3-8228-0266-2

Gestaltung und Redaktion: Gabriele Leuthäuser, Peter
Gössel, Nürnberg
Umschlaggestaltung: Peter Feierabend
English translation: John Bannister, Düsseldorf; Karen
Williams, Köln (captions)
Traduction française: Françoise Laugier-Morun, Essen
Reproduktionen: Werner Pees, Essen; Reprotechnik
Staudacher, Nürnberg
Satz: Utesch Satztechnik GmbH, Hamburg
Druck: Neue Stalling, Oldenburg

Die Übernahme des Textes „The International Style" von
Henry R. Hitchcock and Philip Johnson erfolgt mit freundlicher Genehmigung von W. W. Norton & Company, New
York; die deutsche Übersetzung mit freundlicher Genehmigung des Vieweg Verlags, Wiesbaden.

Abbildung auf dem Umschlag:
Walter Gropius
Toerten, Dessau, 1926–1928
Isometrie 88,8 × 107,3 cm
Busch-Reisinger Museum
Cambridge, Massachusetts

INHALT

CONTENTS

TABLE DES MATIÈRES

VORWORT

Es gab in den dreißiger Jahren verschiedene Ansätze, die vielerorts aktive moderne Architekturbewegung gedanklich zusammenzufassen und die offenkundigen Gemeinsamkeiten des neuen Bauens zu benennen.

Als Henry-Russell Hitchcock und Philip Johnson eine Ausstellung über moderne Architektur im Museum of Modern Art in New York vorbereiteten, die 1932 eröffnet wurde, hatten sie einen Begriff gefunden, der sich hinfort trotz vieler geäußerter Bedenken durchsetzen sollte: »Der Internationale Stil«. Ihrer Meinung nach wies die verbreitete neue Ästhetik der Architektur alle Elemente eines Stils auf, der unabhängig von nationalen Bewegungen umfassend zu beschreiben wäre. Ein Grund für ihre Namensgebung war sicher, daß bis dahin verschiedene »Ismen« kursierten, die weder ausreichend präzise definiert waren noch allgemeingültigen Charakter hatten. So gelang ihnen trotz einer kunsthistorischen Formulierung die Loslösung von der extensiven europäischen Theoriediskussion, in der sich noch Begriffe wie Neoplastizismus, Futurismus, Konstruktivismus und Rationalismus mit »Neuem Bauen« und »Neuer Sachlichkeit« kreuzten.

Eine Rekapitulation dieser Begriffsdiskussion würde den Rahmen dieses Vorworts sprengen, zumal die zeitgenössischen Architekten-Autoren nicht unbedingt in der Konsequenz bauten, in der sie schrieben und darüber hinaus häufig unmittelbaren Bezug zu verwandten Richtungen der bildenden Kunst herzustellen suchten – ein Aspekt wiederum, der hier nicht behandelt werden kann. Dabei unterschied sich der Begriff des Internationalen Stils grundsätzlich von dem des Funktionalismus, ohne aber im beobachteten gebauten Einzelfall unbedingt etwas anderes zu bezeichnen. Es kam eben darauf an, ob man – wie Gropius – seine Auffassung von Architektur von der künstlerischen Sphäre trennen wollte, oder ob man – wie die im entfernten Amerika räsonierenden Johnson und Hitchcock – einen phänomenologischen Blick auf die Architektur warf.

Das funktionalistische Prinzip umreißt an sich den technischen Aspekt der modernen Baukunst und läßt sich rückblickend bereits weit vor den zwanziger Jahren unseres Jahrhunderts ausmachen.

Der Erfolg des Funktionalismusbegriffes setzte aber erst gleichzeitig mit Johnsons und Hitchcocks Stilbegriff ein. Ein wesentlicher Auslöser war das Erscheinen des wohl umfangreichsten Werkes, das aus zeitgenössischer Sicht einen Überblick suchte: »Die Elemente der funktionalen Architektur« von Alberto Sartoris, in der ersten Auflage 1932 erschienen, danach noch zweimal wieder neu herausgegeben. Zuerst hatte Sartoris sein Werk »Die Elemente der rationalen Architektur« genannt, doch – offenbar unter dem Einfluß Le Corbusiers – kam er davon ab und wählte endgültig den neuen Titel. Alberto Sartoris kommentierte seine Zusammenstellung von Hunderten von Bauwerken aus aller Welt wie folgt: »Einen weiteren essentiellen Aspekt des Funktionalismus charakterisiert die Suche nach einem zeitgenössischen Stil mit einheitlichen Konstruktionsverfahren, die aber vielfältige Anwendungen und Interpretationen ermöglichen müssen . . . Die Forderung nach einfachen, nüchternen und nützlichen Formen führt zur Ausbildung einer einheitlichen ästhetischen Richtung . . .« Bis dahin stand das Wort Rationalismus am eindeutigsten für ein Architekturverständnis, das sich im Glauben an eine bessere Gesellschaft vom Prinzip des Individuellen lösen wollte und die Gestaltung in den Dienst des sozialen Fortschritts stellte. Dazu sollten industrielle Bauweisen, ornamentlose Fassaden und standardisierte Pläne beitragen. »Die Wohnung für das Existenzminimum« in großangelegten neuen Siedlungen »mit Licht und Luft für alle« stellte die zentrale Aufgabe in den Zeiten der Wirtschaftskrise dar. Das Bauhaus spielte hier zweifelsohne eine wichtige Rolle, doch das oft gehörte Wort von der »Bauhaus-Architektur« geht völlig an der internationalen Weite der Bewegung vorbei.

Das Bedürfnis, die gemeinsamen Linien herauszuarbeiten und das Verständnis für neue architektonische – und damit unmittelbar verbunden auch stadtplanerische – Ansichten zu wecken, führte auch zur Gründung des »Internationalen Kongresses für Neues Bauen« (Congrès International d'Architecture Moderne). Die gemeinsame Aktivität der Protagonisten in diesem Rahmen ging auf ein Treffen anläßlich der Stuttgarter Werkbundausstellung im Jahr 1927 zurück. Doch das Ziel ging sehr weit, es ging schlechthin um die theoretische Formulierung einer menschengerechten Umwelt in der modernen Industriegesellschaft.

Die gekürzte Fassung des originalen Vorworts des New Yorker Ausstellungskatalogs von 1932 läßt sich als Einführung lesen zu der in diesem Buch vorgelegten Bildfolge, deren Wert darin bestehen mag, unabhängig von Begriffsdiskussionen einen umfassenden Blick auf ein inzwischen historisches architektonisches Phänomen zu werfen. Die Bildfolge steht unter dem Titel »Funktionale Architektur«, da hiermit am deutlichsten die moderne Architekturbewegung vor 1939 umrissen ist. Sie enthält sowohl die wichtigsten Bauwerke, an denen Hitchcock und Johnson ihren neuen Stilbegriff verifizieren wollten, als auch zahlreiche Bauten, die für Sartoris' Bestimmung funktionaler Architektur richtungweisend waren. Sie gibt damit weitgehend den Kenntnisstand des architektonisch interessierten Publikums der dreißiger Jahre wieder und endet mit dem Ausklang dieser Dekade. Schon in der ersten Auflage von Sartoris' Werk schrieb sein Architektenkollege Le Corbusier in Ablehnung der bestehenden Begrifflichkeiten: »Für mich beinhaltet das Wort Architektur etwas Geheimnisvolleres als das Rationale oder das Funktionale, etwas, das herrscht, vorherrscht, sich aufdrängt . . . Es ist zweifelsohne ein menschliches Bedürfnis, warme Füße zu haben; doch meine Sensibilität spricht eher auf ein Bedürfnis an, das auf Harmonie basiert und das mehr wert ist als ein Hummer à l'américain, ein Glas Champagner oder ein frischer Salat . . .«

In the nineteen-thirties, various attempts were made to sum up the thinking behind the modern movement in architecture as it manifested itself in many different places, and to put a name to the common ground evidently shared by the new styles of architecture. During their preparation of an exhibition of modern architecture which opened in the Museum of Modern Art in New York in 1932, Henry Russell Hitchcock and Philip Johnson found an expression which, despite frequently voiced misgivings, was destined to become established from then on: »The International Style«. In their opinion, the widespread new architectural aesthetics contained all the elements of a style which could be comprehensively described without reference to national movements. One reason for their choice of the name was without doubt that up till then various »isms« had been bartered about which were neither adequately precise in their definition nor universally applicable in character. So, despite the fact that they used an art historian's type of expression, they succeeded in breaking away from the extensive European discussion on theory which was still interlaced with expressions such as »Neo-Plasticism«, »Futurism«, »Constructivism«, »Rationalism«, »New Architecture« and »New Functionalism«.

It is not possible to recapitulate the discussion about concepts within the confines of this Foreword, especially since contemporary architect-writers did not always put the same ideas into their writing as they put into practice, and also since they often sought to establish a direct relationship with other art forms – which is another aspect that space does not allow us to examine here.

The concept of the International Style differed fundamentally from that of Functionalism, without however necessarily denoting anything observably different in individual buildings. It all depended on whether – like Gropius – the architect sought to separate his concept of architecture from the world of art, or whether – as in the case of Johnson and Hitchcock's reasoning in far-off America – he preferred to take a phenomenological view of architecture.

The functionalistic principle contains the basic outline of the technical aspect of modern architecture and, in retrospect, can be detected well before the beginning of the nineteen-twenties.

But the success of Functionalism as a term only started around the time of Johnson and Hitchcock's formulation of style. An important catalyst was the appearance of »The Elements of Functional Architecture« by Alberto Sartoris (first edition in 1931, with two further editions since then) which was easily the most comprehensive work of those seeking to provide a contemporary survey. Sartoris had originally called his work »The Elements of Rational Architecture« but, apparently under the influence of Le Corbusier, dropped the idea and finally chose the new title. Alberto Sartoris accompanied his compilation of hundreds of buildings from all round the world with the following comments: »A further essential aspect of Functionalism is characterised by the search for a contemporary style with uniform construction methods which must, however, allow for a wide variety of applications and interpretations ... The requirement for simple, unadorned, utilitarian shapes leads to the development of a uniform aesthetical approach ...«

Up till then, the word »rationalism« had stood most clearly for a concept of architecture which believed in a better society and therefore sought to free itself from the principle of the individual and to put design in the service of social progress. Industrial construction methods, unadorned facades and standardized plans were supposed to contribute towards this. To provide »living accommodation for the minimum level of existence« in large-scale new estates »with light and air for everyone« was the task which presented itself in the years of economic crisis. Without doubt the Bauhaus played an important role in this, yet the frequent references which are made to »Bauhaus architecture« often fail to realise the international scale of the movement.

The need to work out common lines of approach and to awaken understanding for new attitudes towards architecture, and directly related to this, towards town planning, also led to the founding of the »International Congress for New Architecture« (Congrès International d'Architecture Moderne). Cooperation between the protagonists in this context went back to a meeting held on the occasion of the Werkbundausstellung in Stuttgart in 1927. Now, however, far-reaching objectives were set: no less than the theoretical formulation of how the environment should be tailored to fit mankind in the new industrial society. The abridged version of the original foreword to the 1932 New York exhibition catalogue could serve as an introduction to the series of illustrations shown in this book, the value of which is hopefully to provide a survey of what has now become a historical phenomenon in architecture, avoiding discussion of conceptual terminology. The series of illustrations is entitled »Functional Architecture«, as this description most succinctly portrays the modern movement in architecture up to 1939. It contains the most important buildings which Hitchcock and Johnson used as examples to define their new style of architecture, and also a large selection of buildings which paved the way for Sartoris' functional concept of architecture. It therefore provides a wide-ranging reflection of the status of what the architecturally interested public in the thirties was familiar with. It ends with the end of the decade.

In the first edition of Sartoris' book, his fellow architect Le Corbusier dismissed the contemporary preoccupation with conceptual terminology using the following words: »For me the word Architecture contains something much more mysterious than just Rationalism or Functionalism, something which rules and dominates and predominates over everthing else ... Doubtless there exists a human need to have warm feet. But my sensibility shows me a more important need, a need which is based on harmony and is more important than a lobster à l'Americain or a glass of champagne or a fresh salad ...«

PRÉFACE

Dans les années trente, on a assisté à divers essais de résumer mentalement le mouvement moderne agitant l'architecture en de nombreux endroits et de donner un nom aux points communs évidents du nouveau style de construction. C'est en préparant une exposition d'architecture moderne au Museum of Modern Art de New York, qui fut inaugurée en 1932, que Henry-Russell Hitchcock et Philip Johnson trouvèrent un terme qui, malgré les nombreux doutes exprimés, devait par la suite s'imposer: «le Style International». A leur avis, la nouvelle esthétique de l'architecture répandue présentait tous les éléments d'un style que l'on pouvait largement décrire indépendamment des mouvements nationaux. L'une des raisons ayant conduit au choix de ce nom fut certainement aussi que jusqu'à cette époque, on s'était heurté à divers «ismes» qui n'étaient ni définis avec suffisamment de précision, ni ne possédaient un caractère de validité générale. C'est ainsi qu'ils parvinrent à se détacher de la discussion théorique extensive européenne dans laquelle des termes tels que «néoplasticisme», «futurisme», «constructivisme» et «rationalisme» frayaient encore avec la «nouvelle construction» et la «nouvelle objectivité».

Récapituler cette discussion au sujet des termes dépasserait le cadre de cette préface, étant donné que les auteurs contemporains d'architecture n'ont pas forcément appliqué la même conséquence à leurs constructions qu'à leurs écrits, et qu'ils ont en outre souvent tenté d'établir des relations immédiates avec des directions apparentées des arts plastiques – aspect que l'on ne pourra pas traiter ici.

Le terme de Style International se distingue pourtant fondamentalement de celui du fonctionnalisme, sans toutefois nécessairement désigner quelque chose de différent dans le cas particulier de construction observée. Cela dépend en principe de la décision prise à la base: fonder sa conception de l'architecture indépendamment de la sphère artistique – comme Gropius – ou jeter un regard phénoménologique sur l'architecture – comme raisonnèrent Johnson et Hitchcock, en Amérique.

Le principe fonctionnaliste englobe en soi l'aspect technique de l'art architectonique moderne et on peut en retrouver les traces, rétrospectivement, déjà bien avant les années vingt de notre siècle. Le terme de fonctionnalisme ne connut cependant son avènement qu'au moment où apparut le terme de style de Johnson et Hitchcock. L'un des déclencheurs essentiels en fut la parution de l'ouvrage, le plus important sans doute, qui tentait de synthétiser une vue d'ensemble du point de vue contemporain: «Les éléments de l'architecture fonctionnelle» d'Alberto Sartoris, dont la première édition sortit en 1931, pour être ensuite rééditée deux fois. Au début, Sartoris avait intitulé son œuvre «Les éléments de l'Architecture rationnelle», mais manifestement sous l'influence de Le Corbusier – il changea d'idée et choisit définitivement le nouveau titre. C'est de la manière suivante qu'Alberto Sartoris commenta son recueil documentant des centaines de constructions érigées dans le monde entier: «Un autre aspect essentiel du fonctionnalisme est caractérisé par la recherche d'un style contemporain avec des procédés de construction uniformes permettant cependant des applications et des interprétations variées … L'exigence de formes simples, sobres et utiles conduit à la création d'une direction esthétique uniforme …»

Jusqu'à lors, le mot «rationnalisme» avait constitué le terme représentant avec le moins d'équivoque une certaine conception de l'architecture qui, dans sa foi en une société meilleure, voulait se détacher du progrès social. Ainsi, des styles de construction industriels, des façades dépouillées ainsi que des plans standardisés devaient y contribuer. «L'appartement pour le minimum vital» dans de vastes lotissements «avec de la lumière et de l'air pour tous» devint la tâche centrale pendant ces temps de crise économique. Le Bauhaus y joua sans aucun doute un rôle important, mais ce mot si souvent entendu d'«architecture Bauhaus» passe tout à fait à côté de l'ampleur internationale du mouvement.

Le besoin de développer les lignes communes et d'éveiller un sens pour de nouvelles vues architectoniques – et ainsi, en lien direct, aussi concernant l'urbanisme – déboucha également sur la fondation du «Congrès International d'Architecture Moderne». Une rencontre des protagonistes qui s'était déroulée à l'occasion de l'exposition du Werkbund à Stuttgart en 1927 était à l'origine de leur activité commune déployée dans ce cadre. Cependant, l'objectif était très ambitieux, il s'agissait carrément de formuler de manière théorique l'environnement qui serait à la mesure de l'homme dans la société industrielle moderne. La version raccourcie de la préface originale du catalogue d'exposition new-yorkais de 1932 peut être lue en guise d'introduction à la série de reproductions présentées dans ce livre; sa valeur réside peut-être dans le fait qu'elle fournit, indépendamment des discussions concernant la terminologie, une vue détaillée sur un phénomène architectonique entre-temps devenu historique. Cette série de reproductions est intitulée «Architecture fonctionnelle», étant donné que c'est le terme qui caractérise le plus nettement le mouvement d'architecture moderne avant 1939. Elle comprend aussi bien les monuments les plus importants sur lesquels Hitchcock et Johnson voulaient s'appuyer pour vérifier leur nouvelle conception de style, que de nombreux bâtiments qui servirent à Sartoris pour déterminer son architecture fonctionnelle. Elle reflète ainsi largement le niveau de connaissance du public intéressé par l'architecture des années trente, et s'achève à la fin de cette décennie.

Déjà dans la première édition de l'ouvrage de Sartoris, son homologue, l'architecte Le Corbusier, écrit, manifestant son refus envers la terminologie existante: «Pour moi, le mot d'architecture contient quelque chose de plus mystérieux que le rationnel ou le fonctionnel, quelque chose qui règne, domine, s'impose … Avoir les pieds au chaud constitue sans aucun doute un besoin humain; pourtant, ma sensibilité réagit davantage à un besoin fondé sur l'harmonie et qui a plus de valeur qu'un homard à l'américaine, une coupe de champagne ou une salade fraîche …»

DER INTERNATIONALE STIL

THE INTERNATIONAL STYLE

LE STYLE INTERNATIONAL

DER INTERNATIONALE STIL

LE STYLE INTERNATIONAL

Der Stilbegriff, der zu degenerieren begann, als Historismen die Ordnungen des Barock zerstörten, hat wieder Realität und Fruchtbarkeit erlangt. Heute ist die Existenz eines vorherrschenden neuen Stils festzustellen. Die ästhetischen Kategorien, auf denen seine Ordnungskriterien basieren, sind Ergebnisse der Experimente schöpferischer Individualisten. Sie – nicht die Eklektiker – waren die unmittelbaren Leitfiguren derjenigen, die den neuen Stil geschaffen haben. Der Stil unserer Zeit, weltweit verbreitet, ist einheitlich und umfassend, nicht fragmentarisch und widersprüchlich wie so manches Werk der ersten Generation moderner Architekten. In den letzten zehn Jahren hat dieser Stil genügend Bauwerke von Rang hervorgebracht, um seine Gültigkeit und Lebendigkeit unter Beweis stellen zu können. In seiner Bedeutung läßt er sich durchaus mit den Stilen der Vergangenheit vergleichen. In der Behandlung der Probleme der Konstruktion ist er der Gotik verwandt, in der Behandlung der Probleme der Form hat er stärkere Beziehung zur Klassik. In der vorrangigen Behandlung der Funktion steht er über beiden.

Die unkontrollierten und wechselhaften Architekturentwicklungen des 19. Jahrhunderts und die verworrenen und widersprüchlichen Versuche zu Beginn des 20. Jahrhunderts sind nun von einer gerichteten Entwicklung abgelöst worden. Es gibt jetzt eine einheitliche Ordnung, gefestigt genug, um den zeitgenössischen neuen Stil in seiner Existenz zu sichern, und elastisch genug, um individuelle Interpretationen zu erlauben und deren weitere Entwicklung zu ermutigen.

Die Vorstellung, daß Stil eher ein Rahmen für potentielle Entwicklungen sein sollte als eine festgelegte, einengende Form, hat sich mit Blick auf die Prinzipien entfaltet, die die Kunstwissenschaftler als Grundzüge der großen Stile der Vergangenheit erkannt haben. Es sind wenige, aber breit wirksame Prinzipien. Sie beinhalten nicht nur Proportionsregeln, wie bei der Unterscheidung der dorischen von der ionischen Ordnung, sie sind fundamental, wie zum Beispiel die organische Vertikalität der Gotik oder die rhythmische Symmetrie des Barock.

The idea of style, which began to degenerate when the revivals destroyed the disciplines of the Baroque, has become real and fertile again. Today a single new style has come into existence. The aesthetic conceptions on which its disciplines are based derive from the experimentation of the individualists. They and not the revivalists were the immediate masters of those who have created the new style. This contemporary style, which exists throughout the world, is unified and inclusive, not fragmentary and contradictory like so much of the production of the first generation of modern architects. In the decade it has produced sufficient monuments of distinction to display its validity and its vitality. It may fairly be compared in significance with the styles of the past. In the handling of the problems of structure it is related to the Gothic, in the handling of the problems of design it is more akin to the Classical. In the preëminence given to the handling of function it is dinstinguished from both.

The unconscious and halting architectural developments of the nineteenth century, the confused and contradictory experimentation of the beginning of the twentieth, have been succeeded by a directed evolution. There is now a single body of discipline, fixed enough to integrate contemporary style as a reality and yet elastic enough to permit individual interpretation and to encourage general growth.

The idea of style as the frame of potential growth, rather than as archaeologists discern in the great styles of the past. The principles are few and broad. They are not mere formulas of proportion such as distinguish the Doric from the Ionic order; they are fundamental, like the organic verticality of the Gothic or the rhythmical symmetry of the Baroque.

Le concepte de style qui commença à dégénérer lorsque les historismes détruisirent les ordres du Baroque, a de nouveau repris son aspect réel et sa fécondité. De nos jours, on constate l'existence d'un nouveau style dominant. Les catégories esthétiques sur lesquelles ses critères d'ordre se basent, résultent des expériences réalisées par des individualistes créatifs. Ce sont ces derniers – et non pas les éclectiques – qui furent les chefs de file immédiats des créateurs de ce nouveau style. Le style de notre temps, répandu dans le monde entier, est uniforme et étendu, non fragmentaire ni contradictoire comme le sont certaines œuvres issues de la première génération des architectes modernes. Au cours des dix dernières années, ce style a produit assez de monuments de haut rang pour effacer tous les doutes quant à sa validité et sa vivacité. Dans sa signification, il est tout à fait comparable aux styles du passé. Dans le traitement des problèmes de la construction, il est apparenté au Gothique, dans le traitement des problèmes de la forme, il se rapproche davantage du Classique. Quant au traitement prioritaire de la fonction, il est supérieur aux deux.

Désormais, un développement dirigé a pris la relève de l'évolution variable et non contrôlée de l'architecture du XIX⁰ siècle et de ses essais aussi désordonnés que contradictoires du début du XX⁰ siècle. Aujourd'hui, il existe un ordre uniforme qui est assez solide pour assurer le nouveau style contemporain dans son existence et assez élastique pour permettre des interprétations individuelles et pour encourager une poursuite de leur développement.

L'idée selon laquelle le style devrait fournir le cadre permettant des développements potentiels plutôt que de constituer une forme fixe et restreignante, s'est développée en vue des principes que les scientifiques de l'Art ont reconnus comme étant les caractéristiques fondamentales des grands styles du passé. Ces principes sont peu nombreux, mais ont un large rayon d'action. Ils ne contiennent pas seulement des règles de proportions comme dans le cas de la différenciation entre les ordres dorique et ionique, ils sont fondamentaux, comme par exemple la verticalité organique du Gothique ou la symétrie rythmique du Baroque.

Dazu gehört, erstens, das neue Verständnis von Architektur mehr als Raum denn als Masse. Zweitens dient modulare Regelmäßigkeit anstelle von axialer Symmetrie als ordnendes Gestaltungsmittel. Diese beiden Prinzipien kennzeichnen zusammen mit einem dritten, das willkürliche Ornamentierungen verbietet, die Produkte des Internationalen Stils. Dieser neue Stil ist weder international in dem Sinne, daß die Errungenschaften eines Landes genau denen eines anderen gleichen, noch ist er so rigide, daß die Werke verschiedener führender Köpfe sich nicht klar unterscheiden ließen. Der Internationale Stil wurde schrittweise in dem Maße klarer erkennbar und bestimmbar, wie verschiedene Neuerer in der ganzen Welt gleichartige Experimente durchführten.

Funktionalismus

Teilweise kamen die Prinzipien des Internationalen Stils erstmals in den Manifesten zur Sprache, die an der Tagesordnung waren. Teilweise blieben sie unbewußt, so daß es auch heute viel einfacher ist, sie zu spüren, als sie zu erläutern oder in Kategorien zu fassen. Einige der modernen Kritiker und Architekten sowohl in Europa als auch in Amerika leugnen den Rang des ästhetischen Elements in der Architektur, ja sogar dessen Existenz. Alle ästhetischen Stilprinzipien sind für sie bedeutungslos und wirklichkeitsfern. Die neue Auffassung, daß Bauen Wissenschaft sei und keine Kunst, erscheint als eine Überspitzung der Idee des Funktionalismus.
In seiner allgemein bekannten Form ist der Begriff des Funktionalismus dehnbar genug. Er bezieht seine Legitimation sowohl aus der griechischen als auch aus der gotischen Architektur, denn der architektonische Ausdruck basiert beim Tempel genauso wie bei der Kathedrale auf Konstruktion und Funktion. Bei allen Primärstilen der Vergangenheit ist das Ästhetische auf das Technische bezogen, wenn nicht gar von ihm abhängig.

There is, first, a new conception of architecture as volume rather than as mass. Secondly, regularity rather than axial symmetry serves as the chief means of ordering design. These two principles, with a third proscribing arbitrary applied decoration, mark the productions of the international style. This new style is not international in the sense that the production of one country is just like that of another. Nor is it so rigid that the work of various leaders is not clearly distinguishable. The international style has become evident and definable only gradually as different innovators throughout the world have successfully carried out parallel experiments.

Functionalism

In part the principles of the international style were from the first voiced in the manifestoes which were the order of the day. In part they have remained unconscious, so that even now it is far simpler to sense them than to explain them or to state them categorically. Many who appear to follow them, indeed, refuse to admit their validity. Some modern critics and groups of architects both in Europe and in America deny that the aesthetic element in architecture is important, or even that it exists. All aesthetic principles of style are to them meaningless and unreal. This new conception, that building is science and not art, developed as an exaggeration of the idea of functionalism.
In its most generally accepted form the idea of functionalism is sufficiently elastic. It derives its sanctions from both Greek and Gothic architecture, for in the temple as well as in the cathedral the aesthetic expression is based on structure and function. In all the original styles of the past the aesthetic is related to, even dependent on, the technical.

On y compte, premièrement, le fait que la nouvelle conception de l'architecture a davantage lieu au niveau de l'espace que de la masse. Deuxièmement, la régularité modulaire, au lieu de la symétrie axiale, sert de moyen d'organisation esthétique. Ces deux principes marquent, ainsi qu'un troisième qui interdit l'ornementation arbitraire, les produits du Style International. Ce nouveau style n'est pas international dans le sens où les conquêtes d'un pays sont exactement identiques à celles d'un autre, aussi peu qu'il est rigide au point que les œuvres issues de diverses têtes dominantes ne puissent se distinguer les unes des autres. Peu à peu, le Style International est devenu plus clairement reconnaissable et déterminable dans la mesure où divers novateurs, dans le monde entier, ont réalisé des expériences du même type.

Le fonctionnalisme

En partie, les principes du Style International firent pour la première fois leur apparition dans les manifestes qui étaient à l'ordre du jour. Ils demeurèrent partiellement inconscients, de sorte qu'il est plus simple aujourd'hui encore de les ressentir que de les expliquer ou les classer en catégories. Certains des critiques et architectes modernes, aussi bien en Europe qu'en Amérique, nient le haut rang occupé par l'élément esthétique dans l'architecture, et même son existence. Tous les principes esthétiques de style sont insignifiants à leurs yeux et loin de la réalité. La nouvelle conception selon laquelle construire serait une science et non un art apparaît comme outrance de l'idée du fonctionnalisme. Sous sa forme généralement connue, le terme de fonctionnalisme semble être assez extensible. Il puise sa légitimation dans l'architecture aussi bien grècque que gothique, car l'expression architectonique provient, dans le cas du temple comme dans celui de la cathédrale, de la construction et de la fonction. Dans tous les styles primaires du passé, le côté esthétique se réfère au côté technique, quand il n'en est pas carrément dépendant.

Im 19. Jahrhundert waren sowohl die Vertreter des Klassizismus als auch der Neogotik in der Lage, den größten Teil ihres Tuns mit funktionalen Argumenten zu rechtfertigen. Der sogenannte Rationalismus von Architekten wie Schinkel und Labrouste war eine Art von Funktionalismus. Er wurde darüber hinaus nachhaltig durch die kunsthistorische Kritik von Viollet-le-Duc und die ethische Kritik von Pugin und Ruskin verteidigt. Morris und seine Schüler brachten diese Art funktionalistischer Theorie hinüber in unsere Zeit.

Die Doktrin der zeitgenössischen anti-ästhetischen Funktionalisten ist viel strenger. Ihre Grundlage ist eher die Ökonomie als die Ethik oder die Archäologie. Führende europäische Autoren, besonders Sigfried Giedion, vertreten mit einiger Berechtigung den Standpunkt, in der modernen Welt habe Architektur mit so immensen praktischen Problemen zu kämpfen, daß ästhetische Fragen in der Architekturkritik einen sekundären Rang einzunehmen hätten. Architekten wie Hannes Meyer gehen weiter. Sie behaupten, daß das Interesse für Proportionen oder für Gestaltungsprobleme um ihrer selbst willen nur ein unglückseliges Relikt der Ideologie des 19. Jahrhunderts sei. Für Menschen mit einem solchen Verständnis ist es absurd, für den neuen Stil überhaupt Begriffe der Ästhetik zu verwenden. Wenn ein Gebäude angemessen, umfassend und kompromißlos seinem Zweck dient, dann ist es ein gutes Gebäude, unabhängig von seinem Erscheinungsbild. Modernes Bauen bedeutet für sie Geradlinigkeit; sie verwenden, wo immer möglich, standardisierte Teile und vermeiden schmückende oder überflüssige Detaillierung. Jede formale Ausgestaltung, jede nicht notwendige Verwendung besonders herzustellender Teile, jede applizierte Ausschmückung würde die Kosten des Gebäudes erhöhen. Es ist jedoch nahezu unmöglich, ein komplexes Bauwerk zu planen und auszuführen, ohne einige Annahmen zu treffen, die nicht vollständig von Technik und Ökonomie determiniert sind. Man kann deshalb durchaus bezweifeln, daß das von den Intentionen her funktionalistische Bauen überhaupt kein potentiell ästhetisches Element enthält.

The supporters of both the Classical Revival and the Mediaeval Revival in the nineteenth century were ready to defend much of their practice by functionalist arguments. The so-called rationalism of architects like Schinkel and Labrouste was a type of functionalism. It is vigorously advocated, moreover, in the archaeological criticism of Viollet-le-Duc and the ethical criticism of Pugin and Ruskin. Morris and his disciples brought this sort of functionalist theory down to our own day.

The doctrine of the contemporary anti-æsthetic functionalists is much more stringent. Its basis is economic rather than ethical or archaeological. Leading European critics, particularly Siegfried Giedion, claim with some justice that architecture has such immense practical problems to deal with in the modern world that aesthetic questions must take a secondary place in architectural criticism. Architects like Hannes Meyer go further. They claim that interest in proportions or in problems of design for their own sake is still an unfortunate remnant of nineteenth century ideology. For these men it is an absurdity to talk about the modern style in terms of aesthetics at all. If a building provides adequately, completely, and without compromise for its purpose, it is to them a good building, regardless of its appearance. Modern construction receives from them a straightforward expression; they use standardized parts whenever possible and they avoid ornament or unnecessary detail. Any elaboration of design, any unnecessary use of specially made parts, any applied decoration would add to the cost of the building. It is, however, nearly impossible to organize and execute a complicated building without making some choices not wholly determined by technics and economics. One may therefore refuse to admit that intentionally functionalist building is quite without a potential aesthetic element.

Au XIXᵉ siècle, les représentants du style classique aussi bien que ceux du néogothique étaient en mesure de justifier la plus grande partie de leur activité à l'aide d'arguments fonctionnels. Le dit rationalisme réalisé par des architectes tels que Schinkel et Labrouste constituait une sorte de fonctionnalisme. Il fut en outre fortement défendu par la critique de l'histoire de l'art de Viollet-le-Duc et la critique éthique de Pugin et Ruskin. Morris et ses disciples transmirent cette sorte de théorie fonctionnaliste à notre époque.

La doctrine des fonctionnalistes contemporains anti-esthétiques est beaucoup plus sévère. A sa base on trouve davantage l'économie que l'éthique ou l'archéologie. Certains auteurs européens reconnus, notamment Sigfried Giedion, défendent, de manière assez justifiée, le point de vue que dans le monde moderne, l'architecture doit combattre des problèmes pratiques d'une telle envergure que les questions esthétiques devraient prendre un rang secondaire dans la critique de l'architecture. Des architectes tels que Hannes Meyer vont plus loin. Ils prétendent que l'intérêt porté aux proportions ou aux problèmes d'organisation esthétique en eux-mêmes ne constituent que les reliques de l'idéologie du XIXᵉ siècle. Pour ceux qui possèdent une telle conception, il est absurde d'utiliser des termes du domaine de l'esthétique pour le nouveau style. Quand un bâtiment remplit ses fonctions de manière adéquate, complète et sans compromis, c'est un bon bâtiment, indépendamment de son apparence. Construire de manière moderne signifie pour eux des lignes droites: ils utilisent, la où ils le peuvent, des éléments standardisés et évitent les détails décoratifs ou superflus. Toute apparence formelle, toute utilisation non nécessaire de pièces demandant une fabrication spéciale, toute décoration appliquée augmenterait les coûts occasionnés par le bâtiment. Il est toutefois pratiquement impossible de faire les plans et de réaliser un immeuble complexe sans faire quelques exceptions de détails qui ne sont pas totalement déterminés par la technique et l'économie. C'est pourquoi il est légitime de mettre en doute le fait que la construction aux intentions fonctionnelles ne présente absolument aucun élément esthétique potentiel.

Bewußt oder unbewußt muß der Architekt freie Entscheidungen fällen, bevor seine Planung vollendet ist. Bei diesen Entscheidungen folgen die europäischen Funktionalisten eher den Prinzipien des neuen Stils, als daß sie ihnen zuwiderhandeln. Ob sie dies zugeben oder nicht, ist dabei nebensächlich.

In Amerika gibt es ebenfalls Architekten und Autoren, die Architektur nicht, wie in der Vergangenheit, als eine Kunst, sondern eher als eine von vielen Techniken innerhalb der industriellen Zivilisation betrachten. Die ästhetische Beurteilung von Bauwerken scheint ihnen nahezu so bedeutungslos wie die des Straßenbaus. Diese Haltung war in ihrer Auswirkung auf das amerikanische Bauen bis zu einem gewissen Maße nützlich, sogar aus ästhetischer Sicht. Die meisten europäischen Kritiker empfinden ganz richtig, daß die amerikanischen Ingenieure immer viel erfolgreicher mit ihren Techniken umgegangen sind als die amerikanischen Architekten mit ihrer Ästhetik. Die europäischen Funktionalisten sind primär Baumeister und nur unbewußt Architekten. Das hat auch für die Architektur als Kunst seine Vorteile. Kritische Autoren sollten sich über Probleme der Formgebung deutlich ausdrücken können, aber Architekten, deren Ausbildung mehr technischer als intellektueller Natur ist, können es sich leisten, sich der ästhetischen Wirkungen, die sie produzieren, selbst nicht bewußt zu sein. So war es vermutlich auch bei vielen der großen Baumeister der Vergangenheit. Da die Arbeiten der europäischen Funktionalisten sich gewöhnlich innerhalb der Prinzipien des Internationalen Stils bewegen, kann man sie auch als dafür typisch in Anspruch nehmen. Natürlich schaffen diese Doktrinäre seltener Werke herausragender ästhetischer Qualität als diejenigen, die die Kunst der Architektur genauso hingebungsvoll pflegen, wie sie Bauen als Wissenschaft betreiben.

Consciously or unconsciously the architect must make free choices before his design is completed. In these choices the European functionalists follow, rather than go against, the principles of the general contemporary style. Whether they admit it or not is beside the point.

In America also there are both architects and critics who consider architecture not an art, as it has been in the past, but merely a subordinate technic of industrial civilization. Aesthetic criticism of building appears to them nearly as meaningless as aesthetic criticism of road building. Their attitude has been to some extent a beneficial one in its effect on American building, even from the aesthetic point of view. Most European critics feel rightly that American engineers have always been far more successful with their technics than American architects with their aesthetics. The European functionalists are primarily builders, and architects only unconsciously. This has its advantages even for architecture as an art. Critics should be articulate about problems of design; but architects whose training is more technical than intellectual, can afford to be unconscious of the aesthetic effects they produce. So, it may be assumed, were many of the great builders of the past. Since the works of the European functionalists usually fall within the limits of the international style, they may be claimed among its representatives. Naturally these doctrinaires achieve works of aesthetic distinction less often than some others who practice the art of architecture as assiduously as they pursue the science of building.

Consciemment ou inconsciemment, l'architecte doit prendre des décisions libres avant que ses plans soient achevés. Lors de ces décisions, les fonctionnalistes européens observent de préférence les principes du nouveau style plutôt que de les contredire. La question de savoir s'ils l'avouent ou non, est ici d'ordre secondaire.

En Amérique, il existe également des architectes et des auteurs qui considèrent l'architecture non pas, comme dans le passé, comme un art, mais davantage comme l'une des nombreuses techniques faisant partie de la civilisation industrielle. Le jugement esthétique de bâtiments leur paraît pratiquement aussi dénué de sens que celle de la construction de la voirie. Dans une certaine mesure, cette attitude s'est révélée utile du point de vue de son influence sur la construction américaine, et même du point de vue esthétique. La plupart des critiques européens ont le sentiment très juste que les ingénieurs américains ont su tirer bien meilleur parti de leurs techniques que les architectes américains n'ont su le faire de leur notion de l'esthétique.

Les fonctionnalistes européens sont, de façon primaire, des maîtres de la construction et seulement de manière inconsciente des architectes. Ceci présente, aussi pour l'architecture en tant qu'art, des avantages. Les autres critiques devraient savoir s'exprimer clairement au sujet des problèmes de la création de la forme, mais les architectes dont la formation est davantage de nature technique qu'intellectuelle, peuvent se permettre de ne pas être eux-mêmes conscients des effets esthétiques qu'ils produisent. C'est certainement ce qui s'est produit pour la plupart des grands maîtres de la construction du passé. Etant donné que les travaux des fonctionnalistes européens évoluent généralement à l'intérieur des principes du Style International, on peut également les invoquer comme étant typiques en la matière. Evidemment, ces doctrinaires créent plus rarement des œuvres possédant des qualités esthétiques supérieures que ceux qui cultivaient l'art de l'architecture avec autant de passion qu'ils pratiquaient la construction en tant que science.

Es ist nicht nötig, auf die Polemik der Funktionalisten einzugehen, der zufolge es keinen neuen Stil gebe, oder deren eigene Arbeiten als eine andere Art von Architektur zu betrachten. Während die ältere Generation treu am Individualismus festhielt, kam eine Reihe allgemein anwendbarer ästhetischer Prinzipien in Gebrauch. Und während die Funktionalisten daran festhalten, die Bedeutung der ästhetischen Komponente in der Architektur zu leugnen, werden immer mehr Bauwerke errichtet, bei denen diese Prinzipien überlegt, wirksam und ohne Opferung funktionaler Tugenden verfolgt werden.

Ein erstes Prinzip:
Architektur als umschlossener Raum

Die heutigen Bauweisen verwenden als Tragsystem den Rahmen oder das Skelett. Dieses Skelett ist so, wie es vor der Verkleidung des Baus in Erscheinung tritt, jedermann vertraut. Ob das Tragwerk aus Metall ist oder aus bewehrtem Beton, aus der Entfernung wirkt es wie ein Gitter aus Vertikalen und Horizontalen. Zum Schutz gegen die Witterung ist es notwendig, dieses Skelett in irgendeiner Weise mit Wandflächen zu schließen. Im traditionellen Mauerwerksbau waren diese Wände selbst die tragenden Bauteile. Jetzt sind die Wände eher untergeordnete Elemente, die wie dünne Scheiben in das Tragwerk eingepaßt sind oder es wie eine Haut umgeben. So gleicht das Gebäude einem Boot oder einem Regenschirm mit starker innerer Tragstruktur und einer kontinuierlichen äußeren Bedeckung. Bei den Bauten der Vergangenheit übernahm die Wand aus Mauerwerk gleichzeitig sowohl die tragende Funktion als auch den Witterungsschutz. Es ist richtig, daß manchmal noch tragende Mauerwerksscheiben in Verbindung mit Skelettkonstruktionen benutzt werden. Reine Skelette, Tragwerke aus Stahl oder Stahlbeton, sind aber das Normale und Typische.

It is not necessary to accept the contentions of the functionalists that there is no new style or even to consider their own work still another kind of architecture. While the older generation has continued faithful to individualism, a set of general aesthetic principles has come into use. While the functionalists continue to deny that the aesthetic element in architecture is important, more and more buildings are produced in which these principles are wisely and effectively followed without sacrifice of functional virtues.

A first principle:
Architecture as volume

Contemporary methods of construction provide a cage or skeleton of supports. This skeleton as it appears before the building is enclosed is familiar to everyone. Whether the supports are of metal or of reinforced concrete, the effect from a distance is of a grille of verticals and horizontals. For protection against the weather it is necessary that this skeleton should be in some way enclosed by walls. In traditional masonry construction the walls were themselves the supports. Now the walls are merely subordinate elements fitted like screens between the supports or carried like a shell outside of them. Thus the building is like a boat or an umbrella with strong internal support and a continuous outside covering. In the buildings of the past, support and protection were both provided by the same masonry wall. It is true that supporting wall sections are still sometimes used in combination with skeleton construction. Isolated supports, piers of metal or reinforced concrete, are, however, normal and typical.

Il n'est pas nécessaire de s'attarder sur la polémique des fonctionnalistes selon laquelle il n'y aurait pas de nouveau style, ou de considérer leurs propres travaux comme un autre type d'architecture. Alors que l'ancienne génération était restée fidèle à l'individualisme, on se mit à utiler toute une série de principes esthétiques généralement applicables. Et tandis que les fonctionnalistes s'obstinent à nier la signification des composantes esthétiques dans l'architecture, on érige de plus en plus de bâtiments pour lesquels on a suivi ces principes avec beaucoup de réflexion et d'efficacité, sans pour autant faire le sacrifice des vertus fonctionnelles.

Un premier principe:
L'architecture en tant qu'espace enclos

Les modes de construction actuels utilisent comme système de support le cadre ou le squelette. Ce squelette est, tel qu'il apparaît avant la couverture de la construction, familier à chacun. Que la structure portante soit en métal ou en béton, elle produit l'effet, à distance, d'un grillage composé de verticales et d'horizontales. Pour le protéger contre les intempéries, il est nécessaire de recouvrir ce squelette d'une manière quelconque par des surfaces murales. En maçonnerie traditionnelle, ces murs constituaient eux-mêmes les éléments de construction porteurs. De nos jours, les murs représentent davantage des éléments subordonnés que l'on adapte à la structure portante comme de minces tranches ou qui entourent cette dernière comme une peau. C'est ainsi que l'on peut comparer un bâtiment à un bateau ou à un parapluie ayant une forte structure portante intérieure et une couverture extérieure permanente. Dans les bâtiments du passé, le mur de maçonnerie se chargeait autant de la fonction de support que de la protection contre les intempéries. Il est vrai que parfois encore, des tranches de maçonnerie portantes sont utilisées en connexion avec des constructions de squelettes. Cependant, ce sont les purs squelettes, c'est-à-dire les structures portantes d'acier ou de béton, qui constituent le cas normal et typique.

Grundrisse können jetzt mit weit größerer Freiheit behandelt werden als in der Vergangenheit. Die Stützen sind bei modernen Konstruktionen so gering im Durchmesser, daß sie keine ernsthafte Behinderung darstellen. Wenn sie in bestimmten Fällen dennoch stören sollten, können sie auch weggelassen und ihre Lasten von Abfangkonstruktionen aufgenommen werden. In manchen Fällen werden ganze Fassaden durch Kragkonstruktionen so abgefangen, daß die Gebäudehülle in einigem Abstand vor den Stützen verläuft. Die Zeichen moderner Grundrisse haben sich symbolhaft zu Punkten, die Stützen darstellen, und zu Linien als Trennwände und Wetterschutzhaut reduziert. Wir finden nicht mehr die dicken Blöcke und wuchtigen Pfeiler aus tragendem Mauerwerk. Der Grundriß kann fast gänzlich nach den Bedürfnissen, die er erfüllen soll, geplant werden; die Konzessionen, die aus unabdingbaren konstruktiven Gründen gemacht werden müssen, sind minimal.

Die Wirkung von Masse, von statischer Festigkeit, eben noch die primäre Qualität von Architektur, ist verschwunden; an ihre Stelle tritt die Wirkung reiner Körper – oder genauer, von glatten Flächen, die einen Raum umschließen. Das vorherrschende architektonische Element ist nicht mehr der feste Stein, sondern der offene Behälter. In der Tat besteht die große Mehrheit der Gebäude sowohl in der Realität als auch in ihrer Wirkung nur noch aus einfachen Flächen, die einen Raum umschließen. Mit der lediglich durch eine Schutzhaut umhüllten Skelettkonstruktion kann es der Architekt kaum vermeiden, diese Wirkung des durch ebene Oberflächen umschlossenen Volumens zu erzielen, es sei denn, er verläßt seinen Weg, um aus Respekt vor der traditionellen Formgebung mit den Regeln der Massivität einen gegensätzlichen Effekt zu erzielen.

Die europäischen Funktionalisten stimmen unausgesprochen mit diesem Ziel des Internationalen Stils überein, ohne dessen Wert als ästhetischen Ordnungsfaktor zu akzeptieren.

Plans may be worked out with far greater freedom than in the past. The piers of modern construction are so slight in section that they create no serious obstruction. If in given cases they might interfere, occasional supports may be omitted and their burden carried by cantilevering. Entire façades are frequently cantilevered and the screen walls set some distance outside the supports. Symbolically the indication of modern plans is reduced to points representing support and lines representing separation and protection from the weather. No longer do we find the solid blocks of bearing walls and piers of masonry. The plan can be composed almost entirely in terms of the needs it must provide for, with only minimal concessions to the inescapable needs of sound construction.

The effect of mass, of static solidity, hitherto the prime quality of architecture, has all but disappeared; in its place there is an effect of volume, or more accurately, of plane surfaces bounding a volume. The prime architectural symbol is no longer the dense brick but the open box. Indeed, the great majority of buildings are in reality, as well as in effect, mere planes surrounding a volume. With skeleton construction enveloped only by a protective screen, the architect can hardly avoid achieving this effect of surface of volume unless, in deference to traditional design in terms of mass, he goes out of his way to obtain the contrary effect.

The European functionalists conform unconsciously to this principle of the international style without accepting its validity as an aesthetic discipline.

Désormais, on peut réaliser les plans avec plus de liberté que dans le passé. Les colonnes ont un diamètre tellement réduit dans les constructions modernes qu'elles ne constituent plus de handicap sérieux. Si dans certains cas, elles sont toutefois gênantes, on peut les supprimer totalement et reporter la charge sur des constructions d'étaiement. Dans certains cas, des façades complètes sont étayées par des constructions en porte-à-faux de telle manière que le mur rideau du bâtiment se dresse à une certaine distance devant les colonnes. Les dessins des plans modernes se sont symboliquement réduits à des points représentant les colonnes, et à des lignes indiquant les cloisons séparatrices et le mur rideau protégeant contre les intempéries. Nous ne trouvons plus les blocs épais ni les puissants piliers formés dans la maçonnerie d'étaiement. Le tracé au sol peut être presque totalement déterminé en fonction des besoins auxquels il est censé répondre; les concessions que l'on doit faire pour des raisons de nécessité absolue liées à la construction sont minimales.

L'effet de masse, de solidité statique, c'est-à-dire encore la qualité primaire de l'architecture, a disparu; à sa place, on voit apparaître l'effet de corps purs – ou plus exactement, de surfaces lisses englobant un espace. L'élément architectonique dominant n'est plus la pierre solide mais le récipient ouvert. En effet, la grande majorité des bâtiments ne se composent plus, aussi bien en réalité que dans leur effet, que de surfaces simples englobant un espace. A l'aide de la construction d'un squelette simplement enveloppé d'un mur protecteur, l'architecte ne peut guère éviter d'atteindre cet effet de volume enclos entre des surfaces planes, à moins que, par respect de la création traditionnelle des formes, il ne délaisse son objectif pour tenter d'atteindre un effet contraire aux règles de la massivité.

Les fonctionnalistes européens sont absolument unanimes quant à ce but du Style International, sans pour autant en accepter la valeur en tant que facteur d'ordre esthétique.

Die amerikanischen Funktionalisten dagegen überladen häufig ihre Fassaden, obwohl der Effekt von Gewicht und Solidität den nichttragenden Charakter ihrer Vorhangfassaden verdeckt. Wenn sie überhaupt gestalten – außer bei Fabriken verlangt der Auftraggeber in der Regel irgendein appliziertes Design –, dann gestalten sie nach Art des Massivbaus. Jeder kennt den verblüffenden Gegensatz, den ein Gebäude während der Bauzeit bietet: das kraftvolle, leichte Gerüst aus Stahl und die schweren, massig wirkenden Fassadenteile, mit denen es schon teilweise verkleidet ist. Die wachsende Einfachheit neuerer Wolkenkratzer, die Vergrößerung der Fensterflächen und der ansteigende Wissensstand vom Internationalen Stil sind Faktoren, die diese oberflächliche Schwere nun nach und nach reduzieren. Aber immer noch gilt: Je teurer ein Gebäude ist, desto sicherer besteht ein Konflikt zwischen seinem wahren Charakter als verkleidetem Stahlgerüst und der wahrnehmbaren Massivität seiner vertikalen Stützen und seines pyramidenförmigen Aufbaus. Die großen Stile der Vergangenheit bestehen aus mehr als einer bestimmten Art von Baukonstruktion oder einem bestimmten Repertoire an Ornamenten. Säulen- und Balkenkonstruktionen wurden sowohl in der ägyptischen als auch in der griechischen Architektur benutzt. Romanische Kirchen setzten ein nahezu gleich weit entwickeltes Wissen und Können in der Gewölbetechnik voraus wie die späteren Kirchen der Gotik. Die gotischen Baumeister betonten die Wirkung von Höhe und von regelhafter Vielfalt organisch einander zugeordneter Teile; die griechischen Architekten gestalteten ihre Architektur so, daß ihre Bauten den körperlich-plastischen Charakter ihrer Skulpturen erhielten. Stil ist Charakter, Stil ist Ausdruck; aber auch Charakter muß entfaltet werden, und Ausdruck kann bewußt und klar erzielt werden oder auf unklare und täuschende Art.

The American functionalists, however, often load their surfaces, thus obscuring with an effect of solidity and weight the non-supporting character of their wall screens. If the design at all – and except in factories the client usually demands some sort of applied design – they design still in mass. A striking contrast is familiar to everyone as it appears in buildings under construction: the strong light cage of steel, and the heavy solid-appearing walls with which it is gradually covered. The greater simplicity of the newer skyscrapers, the increase in the window area and the growing awareness of the international style are reducing little by little this superficial heaviness. But thus far the more expensive the building, the more surely is there a conflict between its true character as an enclosed steel cage and the apparent mass of its vertical buttressing and its pyramidal composition.

In the past the great styles became something more than a certain sort of construction, or a certain repertory of ornament. Post and lintel construction was used in Egyptian architecture as well as Greek. Romanesque churches achieved nearly as great a science and elaboration of vaulting as did the later ones of the Gothic age. The Gothic architects emphasized the impression of height and or orderly multiplicity of organically related parts; the Greek architects so adjusted their design as to give their buildings the plastic somatic character of their sculpture. Style is character, style is expression; but even character must be displayed and expression may be conscious and clear, or muddled and deceptive.

Les fonctionnalistes américains en revanche surchargent souvent leurs façades, bien que l'effet de poids et de solidité ne compense pas le caractère non porteur de leur façades rideaux. Quand ils créent une décoration – mis à part le cas d'usines, le commettant demande en règle générale un quelconque design appliqué –, ils composent à la manière d'une construction massive. Chacun connaît le contraste stupéfiant que présente un bâtiment pendant sa construction: la charpente puissante, mais légère d'acier, à côté des lourds éléments de la façade, à l'aspect si massif, dont elle est déjà recouverte en partie. La simplicité croissante des nouveaux gratte-ciel, l'agrandissement des surfaces de fenêtres et l'élévation du niveau de connaissances du Style International constituent des facteurs qui tendent actuellement à réduire peu à peu cette lourdeur superficielle. Toutefois, ceci est toujours valable: plus un bâtiment est cher, plus il est sûr qu'il y aura un conflit entre son vrai caractère de charpente d'acier recouverte et la massivité perceptible de ses colonnes verticales et de sa structure pyramidale.

Les grands styles du passé se composent de plus d'une sorte particulière de construction de bâtiments ou d'un répertoire particulier d'ornements. Les constructions à colonnes et à poutres furent utilisées dans les architectures aussi bien égyptienne que grècque. Les églises romanes exigeaient un savoir et une habileté presque aussi développés au niveau de la technique des voûtes que les églises construites plus tard à l'époque du Gothique. Les maîtres d'œuvre gothiques accentuèrent l'effet de hauteur et de diversité régulière des éléments reliés organiquement les uns aux autres; les architectes grecs composèrent leur architecture de telle manière que leurs bâtiments revêtent le même caractère de corps plastique que leurs sculptures. Le style est caractère, le style est expression; mais le caractère doit lui aussi être développé et l'expression peut être obtenue consciemment et clairement ou de manière trouble et trompeuse.

Der Architekt, der im Internationalen Stil baut, arbeitet darauf hin, den wahren Charakter seines Baus zu entfalten und die Erfüllung der Funktion klar auszudrücken. Er erstrebt eine Organisation des Gesamtaufbaus, einen Gebrauch von verfügbaren Materialien und eine Handhabung von Details, dergestalt, daß die primäre Wirkung eines von glatten Flächen umschlossenen Raums eher gesteigert als gestört wird.

Um diese Wirkung zu erzielen, sind flache, für moderne Bauweisen geeignete Dächer von wesentlicher ästhetischer Bedeutung. Pultdächer sind dennoch gelegentlich mit Erfolg verwendet worden. Denn sie wirken leichter und einfacher als die Sattel- und Walmdächer der Gebäude der Vergangenheit. Flachdächer sind so viel nützlicher, daß geneigte oder tonnenförmige Dächer nur ausnahmsweise berechtigt sind.

Die Klarheit der Erscheinung des reinen Volumens wird durch jede Art Störung gemindert. Das reine Volumen wird als immateriell und gewichtslos empfunden, als geometrisch bestimmter Raum. Als Anbauten konzipierte Teile eines Gebäudes neigen dazu, massiv zu erscheinen. Deshalb dürfte eine kompakte und einheitliche Lösung eines Problems sowohl ästhetisch als auch ökonomisch am besten sein. Die Massivität der Architektur der Vergangenheit – Oberfläche und Inhalt wirken zusammen – wird als schwer empfunden. Wegen ihrer Schwere paßt zu massiver Architektur ein Erscheinungsbild des Lastentragens, wie es zum Beispiel bei aufeinandergetürmten Teilen gegeben ist. Diese Art von Stabilität, gleich der eines Holzstapels, vermittelt unsere grazile Gitterbauweise nicht. Die Sinnhaftigkeit des inneren Tragwerks wird hingegen mit dem Weglassen untergeordneter Teile und dem Erzielen eines möglichst reinen Körpers mit gleichartigen Oberflächen noch gesteigert.

The architect who builds in the international style seeks to display the true character of his construction and to express clearly his provision for function. He prefers such an organization of his general composition, such a use of available surface materials, and such a handling of detail as will increase rather than contradict the prime effect of surface of volume.

In giving this effect the flat roofs normal with modern methods of construction have an essential aesthetic significance. Roofs with a single slant, however, have occasinaly been used with success. For they are less massive and simpler than the gabled roofs usual on the buildings of the past. Flat roofs are so much more useful that slanting or rounded roofs are only exceptionally justified.

The clarity of the impression of volume is diminished by any sort of complication. Volume is felt as immaterial and weightless, a geometrically bounded space. Subsidiary projecting parts of a building are likely to appear solid. Hence a compact and unified solution of a complex problem will be best aesthetically as well as economically. The massiveness of the architecture of the past was felt as gravitational, with surface and content one. Being heavy, massive architecture demanded the appearance of support such as could be given by a piling up of the parts. This sort of stability, like that of a wood pile, our tenuous cage construction does not give. The sense of internal support is, on the other hand, increased by the avoidance of subsidiary parts and by the achievement as far as possible of the effect of a single volume with continuous surfaces.

L'architecte qui construit selon le Style International travaille afin de déployer le caractère véritable de sa construction et d'exprimer clairement la réponse à une fonction donnée. Il aspire à une organisation de l'ensemble de la construction, une utilisation de matériaux disponibles et une mise en œuvre des détails telle que l'effet primaire d'un espace enclos entre des surfaces lisses soit davantage augmenté que détruit. Pour atteindre cet effet, les toits plats, adaptés aux constructions modernes, possèdent une signification esthétique essentielle. Cependant, les toits à une pente ont été à l'occasion utilisés avec succès. Car ils produisent l'impression d'être plus légers et plus simples que les toits à deux ou à quatre versants des bâtiments du passé. Les toits plats sont tellement plus utiles, que ce n'est que de manière exceptionnelle que l'on peut justifier les toits pentus ou les toits-voûtes.

La clarté de l'apparition du pur volume est diminuée par chaque sorte d'interférence. Le pur volume semble immatériel et sans masse, un espace géométriquement déterminé. Les parties d'un bâtiment conçues en tant qu'annexe tendent à paraître massives. C'est pourquoi il semble que la solution compacte et uniforme d'un problème soit la meilleure, aussi bien sur le plan esthétique que du point de vue économique. La massivité de l'architecture du passé – surface et contenu produisent un effet commun – est ressentie comme lourde. A cause de sa lourdeur, on associe à l'architecture massive une image de porteur de charge, comme on peut l'observer par exemple dans le cas d'éléments empilés. Cette sorte de solidité, ressemblant à celle d'une pile de bois, n'est pas diffusée par notre gracile mode de construction à charpente grillagée. La signification de la structure portante interne est en revanche encore accrue par la suppression des éléments subordonnés et par l'atteinte d'un corps aussi pur que possible comprenant des surfaces de même nature.

Wie eine natürliche Folge des Prinzips des von Flächen umschlossenen Raums ergibt sich als weitere Forderung, daß die Oberflächen in ihrer Wirkung nicht unterbrochen sein sollten, wie die leicht gespannte Haut über dem stützenden Skelett. Die in Erscheinung tretenden Kräfte bei einer gemauerten Wand entsprechen direkt der Schwerkraft, obwohl ihre Ableitung in Wirklichkeit durch den Gebrauch von Stützen und Bögen mehr oder weniger modifiziert wird. Die bei Vorhangfassaden in Erscheinung tretenden Kräfte sind nicht in dieser Weise senkrecht gerichtet, sondern werden als in alle Richtungen gehend empfunden, ganz wie bei einem gespannten Textilgewebe. Deshalb ist die Unterbrechung der Fassadenoberfläche durch innen angeordnete (statt außen bündig liegende) Fenster wirklich ein architektonischer Fehler. Denn das Glas der Fenster ist jetzt, anders als beim Mauerwerksbau, wo es wie ein Loch in der Wand wirkt, ein integrierter Teil der Außenhaut.

Heutige Bauten haben oft gänzlich transparente Außenwände aus Glas, die ein einziges, riesiges Fenster bilden. Die Sprossen der Glasfelder solcher Fassaden müssen so dünn sein, daß sie sich von echten Tragelementen unterscheiden, weil sonst die untergeordneten Gliederungen die Fläche so stark in einzelne Felder teilen würden, daß ihr kontinuierlicher Charakter verloren ginge. Obwohl das Tragskelett dahinter klar zu sehen wäre, würden solche Teilungen zu einem Eindruck von Gewichtigkeit, wenn nicht von Masse führen. Es ist keineswegs immer einfach für den Architekten, solche völlig transparenten Außenwände wirkungsvoll zu lösen. Sie scheinen nicht mehr das Extrem zu sein, zu dem die Entwicklung des heutigen Stils unvermeidlich hinführt. Dennoch war, wie der Kristallpalast aus dem letzten Jahrhundert und die Stahl-Glas-Kaufhäuser von 1900 zeigen, eine derartige Maximalverglasung eine Vorbereitung für die Entwicklung eines allgemeingültigeren Prinzips der modernen Architektur: das der Betonung der Fläche, sei sie nun undurchsichtig oder transparent.

Thus as a corollary of the principle of surface of volume there is the further requirement that the surfaces shall be unbroken in effect, like a skin tightly stretched over the supporting skeleton. The apparent tensions of a masonry wall are directly gravitational, although they are actually modified more or less by the use of lintels and arches. The apparent tensions of screen walls are not thus polarized in a vertical direction, but are felt to exist in all directions, as in a stretched textile. Hence the breaking of the wall surface by placing windows at the inner instead of a the outer edge of the wall is a serious fault of design. For the glass of the windows is now an integral part of the enclosing screen rather than a hole in the wall as it was in masonry construction.

Contemporary buildings often have entire walls of transparent glass constituting one enormous window. The frames of the panes in such walls must be light enough to be distinguished from true supports. Otherwise these subordinate divisions will so break up the surface into panels that its continuous character is confused. Even though the independent supporting skeleton is perfectly clearly seen behind, such a panelled treatment appears to have weight if not mass. Such altogether transparent walls are not by any means the easiest for the architect to handle effectively. They no longer appear the extreme toward which the development of the contemporary style inevitably leads. Indeed, as the Crystal Palace of the last century and the steel and glass department stores of 1900 suggest, such maximal fenestration was a preparation for the development of a more general principle of modern design: that of emphasizing the surfaces whether they are opaque or transparent.

Conséquence naturelle du principe de l'espace entouré de surfaces, l'exigence suivante est que les surfaces ne doivent pas être interrompues dans leur effet, comme la peau légèrement tendue sur le squelette de support. Les forces apparaissant au niveau d'un mur de maçonnerie correspondent directement à la pesanteur, bien que leur dérivation soit en réalité plus ou moins modifiée par l'utilisation de colonnes et d'arcs. Les forces apparaissant dans le cas de façades rideaux ne sont pas dirigées à la verticale de cette manière, mais sont ressenties dans tous les sens, tout à fait comme pour un tissu textile tendu. C'est pourquoi l'interruption de la surface de la façade par une fenêtre ordonnée par l'intérieur (et non alignée sur l'extérieur) constitue vraiment une erreur architectonique. Car le verre de la fenêtre est maintenant, autrement que dans la construction de murs de maçonnerie où il produit l'effet d'un trou dans le mur, une partie intégrante de l'enveloppe extérieure.

Les constructions actuelles présentent souvent des murs extérieurs de verre complètement transparents, formant une immense fenêtre unique. Les traverses des surfaces de verre de telles façades doivent être si minces qu'elles se distinguent des vrais éléments porteurs, parce que sinon, les éléments subordonnés partageraient la surface en tellement de champs distincts que son caractère continu disparaîtrait. Bien que le squelette porteur soit clairement visible derrière cette surface, de telles interruptions provoqueraient une impression de lourdeur, si ce n'est de masse. Il n'est pas toujours facile, pour un architecte, de trouver une solution qui produise de l'effet, à ces murs extérieurs complètement transparents. Ceux-ci ne semblent plus représenter cet extrême sur lequel le développement du style actuel débouche inévitablement. Pourtant, une telle vitrification maximale joua le rôle, comme le montrent le palais de cristal du siècle dernier et les grands magasins de verre et d'acier, une préparation au développement d'un principe universellement valable dans l'architecture moderne: celui de l'accentuation de la surface, qu'elle soit opaque ou transparente.

Der Geist des Prinzips der glatten Flächen schließt viele Beispiele ein, die Ausnahmen wären, wenn man wortwörtlich vorginge. Der Bautyp, den Mies van der Rohes Barcelona-Pavillon repräsentiert, führt ebenso wie derjenige, der sich in Le Corbusiers Haus in Le Pradet manifestiert, zu einer Behandlung von Flächen, die spürbar anders ist als jene, die hier vor allem hervorgehoben wurde. Nichtsdestoweniger bezeugen diese Werke, daß ihre Architekten die Möglichkeiten des Stils unserer Zeit erweitern. In beiden Bauwerken werden Flächen betont, die ungebrochen sind, obwohl ihre Beziehung zu den tragenden Bauteilen nicht so eindeutig ist wie bei den meisten Gebäuden.

Das Prinzip des flächenumschlossenen Raums wird, intelligent interpretiert, immer dort zu besonderen Anwendungen führen, wo die Konstruktion nicht das typische, von einer Schutzhaut umgebene Gitter oder Skelett ist. Die offensichtliche Ausnahme kann nicht die Gültigkeit des allgemeinen Prinzips in Frage stellen, zeigt jedoch unübersehbar dessen Elastizität. Feste Gestaltungsregeln werden trotz ihrer Rigidität schnell durchbrochen; elastische Architekturprinzipien wachsen und entfalten sich. Weder die Ursprünge bestimmter Bauweisen noch die allzeit gebotenen verschiedenartigen Möglichkeiten vergessend, sollten Architekten in Prinzipien wie dem des flächenumschlossenen Raums eine sichere und dauerhafte Anleitung finden, wie sie der Internationale Stil entwickelt.

Ein zweites Prinzip: Bemühung um modulare Regelmäßigkeit

Das Maßwerk gotischer Fenster stützte sich in seiner Ordnung auf klare Gestaltungsprinzipien, die aus der Baustruktur abgeleitet waren, und entwickelte sich erst nach und nach zu freiem Schmuckwerk. Vorausgesetzt, heute existierte ein verbindlicher Stil, so müssen sich die Unterteilungen der Fenster und die Zuordnung der Bestandteile zeitgenössischer Architektur ebenfalls auf ein ästhetisches Prinzip stützen.

The spirit of the principle of surface covers many exceptions to its letter. The type of construction represented by Miës van de Rohe's Barcelona pavilon, as well as that represented in Le Corbusiers's house at Le Pradet, leads to a treatment of surfaces sensibly different from that which has been primarily stressed here. These works, nevertheless, testify that their designers are extending the possibilities of the contemporary style. In each of these buildings the surfaces are emphasized and their continuity made evident although their relation to the supporting construction is less simple than in most buildings.

The principle of surface of volume intelligently understood will always lead to special applications where the construction is not the typical cage or skeleton of supports surrounded by a protecting screen. The apparent exception may not prove the validity of the general principle, but its undoubtedly indicates its elasticity. Rigid rules of design are easily broken once and for all; elastic principles of architecture grow and flourish. Forgetting neither the origins in a certain type of construction nor the possibilities which lie always ahead architects should find in such principles as that of surface of volume a sure and continuing guidance as the international style develops.

A second principle: Concerning regularity

The patterns of Gothic fenestration were ordered according to definite conceptions of design derived from structure and leading more and more to arbitrary decoration. Today the patterns of windows, the composition of the parts of contemporary architecture, must also be ordered according to an aesthetic principle if a contemporary style exist.

L'esprit du principe des surfaces lisses comprend beaucoup d'exemples qui constituaient des exceptions si on agissait en suivant la théorie au pied de la lettre. Le type de construction que représente le pavillon de Barcelone de Mies van der Rohe, mène tout autant que celui qui se présente en la maison de Le Corbusier au Pradet à un traitement des surfaces sensiblement différent de celui qui a été ici particulièrement mis en valeur. Néanmoins, ces œuvres prouvent que leurs architectes élargissent les possibilités du style de notre temps. Dans ces deux bâtiments, les surfaces ininterrompues sont accentuées, bien que leurs rapports avec les parties portantes de la construction ne soient pas aussi évidents que dans la plupart des bâtiments.

Le principe de l'espace enfermé entre des surfaces conduira toujours, s'il est interprété intelligemment, à des applications originales là où la construction n'est pas un grillage ou squelette typique entouré d'une façade rideau. L'exception évidente ne peut mettre en doute la validité du principe général, mais en montre l'élasticité indéniable. Les règles fixes de composition peuvent être rapidement bouleversées, malgré leur rigidité; quant aux principes élastiques d'architecture, ils croissent et s'épanouissent. En n'oubliant ni les origines de certains modes de construction, ni les possibilités les plus diverses s'offrant de tout temps, les architectes devraient trouver des instructions sûres et durables dans des principes tels que celui de l'espace enclos entre des surfaces, telles que les développe de Style International.

Un second principe: La recherche d'une régularité modulaire

L'œuvre type des fenêtres gothiques se basait, dans son ordre, sur des principes de composition clairs qui avaient été dérivés de la structure de construction, et ne se développa que peu à peu en un libre ouvrage de décoration. A condition qu'il existe aujourd'hui un style obligatoire, les subdivisions des fenêtres et l'ordre des parties composant l'architecture contemporaire devraient également s'appuyer sur un principe esthétique.

Die Funktionalisten behaupten, daß sie ihre Entwürfe allein auf praktischen Erfordernissen aufbauen. Aber auch sie akzeptieren wegen des wirtschaftlichen Zwangs zur Standardisierung eine Entwurfsdisziplin, die man ganz ähnlich im Werk derjenigen zeitgenössischen Architekten findet, die die Bedeutung ästhetischer Beweggründe anerkennen. Neben dem Prinzip des flächig umschlossenen Raums gibt es ein zweites Grundprinzip, das in den Schöpfungen des Internationalen Stils unter Einschluß der Arbeiten der europäischen Funktionalisten deutlich hervortritt. Dieses zweite Prinzip des heutigen Architekturstils hat mit modularer Regelmäßigkeit zu tun. Stützen von Skelettkonstruktionen sind in der Regel in gleichen Abständen angeordnet, um keine unterschiedlichen Spannweiten zu bekommen. Deshalb liegt den meisten Gebäuden ein regelmäßiger Rhythmus zugrunde, was deutlich zu sehen ist, solange die Außenverkleidung noch nicht montiert ist. Außerdem legen wirtschaftliche Erwägungen die durchgängige Verwendung standardisierter Teile nahe. Gute moderne Architektur weist in ihrem Erscheinungsbild jene charakteristische Rasterung der Baustruktur mit gleichartigen Teilen auf, die durch ihre ästhetische Ordnung die Regelmäßigkeit des zugrundeliegenden Tragwerks betont. Schlechte moderne Entwürfe mißachten diese Regelmäßigkeit. Regelmäßigkeit in der Architektur ist jedoch relativ, nicht absolut.

Den unterschiedlichen Aufgaben, denen die meisten Gebäude dienen, kann nicht vollständig durch modulare Regelmäßigkeit entsprochen werden. Ein Hochhaus in der Stadt könnte – und dies ist oft der Fall – regelmäßig strukturiert sein, wenn man von Eingangszonen und Aufzugsgruppen absieht. Die Zwecke, denen jedes Geschoß dient, sind einander so ähnlich, daß überall der gleiche Grundriß und Schnitt verwendet werden kann. Jedoch sind nur wenige Gebäudearten von solcher Einfachheit.

The functionalists claim that they order their designs according to practical considerations alone. Yet even they, because of the economic force of standardization, accept a discipline of design not dissimilar to that found in the work of contemporary architects who grant the importance of aesthetic considerations. Beside the principle of surface of volume already discussed there is a second controlling principle, evident in the productions of the international style including the work of the European functionalists.

This second principle of contemporary style in architecture has to do with regularity. The supports in skeleton construction are normally and typically spaced at equal distances in order that strains may be equalized. Thus most buildings have an underlying regular rhythm which is clearly seen before the outside surfaces are applied. Moreover, economic considerations favor the use of standardized parts throughout. Good modern architecture expresses in its design this characteristic orderliness of structure and this similarity of parts by an aesthetic ordering which emphasizes the underlying regularity. Bad modern design contradicts this regularity. Regularity is, however, relative and not absolute in architecture.

The varied purposes which most buildings serve cannot be completely regularized. A loft building in a city may be, and often is, regular throughout except for the entrances and the elevators. The many purposes which each floor serves are so nearly alike that the same plan and elevation may be used throughout. Few buildings, however, are so simple.

Les fonctionnalistes prétendent qu'ils n'élaborent leurs plans que sur la base de nécessités pratiques. Mais eux aussi acceptent, en raison des contraintes économiques qui forcent à standardiser, une discipline au niveau de l'élaboration du projet, discipline que l'on retrouve sous une forme analogue dans l'œuvre de ces architectes contemporains qui reconnaissent la signification des motifs esthétiques. Outre le principe de l'espace enclos entre des surfaces, il existe un deuxième principe de base qui apparaît clairement dans les créations du Style International en incluant les travaux des fonctionnalistes européens. Ce deuxième principe du style de l'architecture actuelle est relié à la régularité modulaire. Les colonnes des constructions de squelettes sont en règle générale ordonnées à intervalles réguliers pour éviter d'obtenir des archées différentes. C'est pourquoi on trouve à la base de la plupart des bâtiments un rythme régulier, chose que l'on observe nettement tant que la couverture extérieure n'est pas encore installée. En outre, des considérations économiques justifient l'utilisation conséquente d'éléments standardisés. La bonne architecture moderne présente, dans son apparence, ce quadrillage caractéristique de la structure de construction en partie de même nature, accentuant par leur ordre esthétique la régularité de la structure de support se trouvant à la base. Les mauvais plans modernes négligent cette régularité. Cependant, la régularité dans l'architecture est relative, et non absolue. Il n'est pas possible de répondre complètement à tous les devoirs, auxquels servent la plupart des bâtiments, par la régularité modulaire. Une tour située en pleine ville pourrait – et ceci est souvent le cas – être structurée avec régularité, si l'on fait abstraction des zones d'entrée et des groupes d'ascenseurs. Les utilisations auxquelles on destine chaque étage se ressemblent tellement entre elles que l'on peut partout utiliser la même coupe et le même plan. Cependant, il n'existe que très peu de types de bâtiments possédant une telle simplicité.

In den meisten Fällen muß der Architekt innerhalb einer Struktur, die unter Benutzung gleichartiger Teile möglichst regelmäßig ausgebildet ist, viele variierende Funktionen erfüllen, die auf unterschiedliche Weise aufeinander bezogen sind. Annäherungen an absolute Regelmäßigkeiten sind auch Annäherungen an Monotonie, was man am angeführten Beispiel des Hochhauses in der Stadt schon gesehen haben mag. Das Prinzip der modularen Regelmäßigkeit verweist eher auf eine Art des Ordnens und auf ein Mittel, einem Architekturentwurf eine definierte Form zu geben, als auf ein endgültiges Ziel, das für sich steht. Letztendlich unterliegt die Regelmäßigkeit der gleichen Notwendigkeit wie jede ästhetische Gestaltung, nämlich der, ein angemessenes Maß an Bedeutung zu erlangen. Was dieses Maß an Bedeutsamkeit ausmacht, ist theoretisch kaum zu definieren.

In den verschiedenen Stilen der Vergangenheit war die Architektur eher dem Prinzip der Axialsymmetrie unterworfen als dem der Regelmäßigkeit, wie wir es verstehen. Die griechische Bedeutung von Symmetrie, »das rechte Verhältnis der verschiedenen Teile zueinander«, ist nahezu deckungsgleich mit dieser besonderen Bedeutung von Regelmäßigkeit. Die griechische Symmetrie war aber gewöhnlich sowohl spiegelgleich als auch regelmäßig. Axialsymmetrie wurde im allgemeinen dazu benutzt, wie in der Barock-Architektur die Ordnung von Unregelmäßigkeit zu bewerkstelligen und die Konfusion voneinander unabhängiger Bestandteile und reich ausgearbeiteter Details zu beherrschen und zu verknüpfen. Moderne Standardisierung ergibt von selbst einen hohen Grad von Stimmigkeit der einzelnen Teile. Darum benötigen moderne Architekten nicht die Disziplin der Spiegelgleichheit oder Axialsymmetrie, um ästhetische Ordnung zu erzielen.

In most cases, within a structure as regular as possible and using similar parts the architect must provide for many varying functions related in various different ways to one another.

It must be remembered that the nearer approaches to absolute regularity are also approaches to monotony, as the earlier reference to the loft building will have suggested. The principle of regularity refers to a means of organization, a way of giving definite form to an architectural design, rather than to an end which is sought for itself. As an end, regularity is modified by the equal necessity, understood in all aesthetic organization, of achieving a proper degree of interest. What constitutes a proper degree of interest is hardly to be determined in theory.

In the various styles of the past a principle of axial symmetry controlled design rather than a principle of regularity as that is understood here. The Greek meaning of symmetry, »a due proportion of the several parts,« was nearly equivalent to this special meaning of regularity. But Greek symmetry was usually bilateral as well as regular. Axial symmetry has generally been used to achieve the ordering of irregularity, as in Baroque architecture, dominating and relating the confusion of independent features and elaborate detail. Modern standardization gives automatically a high degree of consistency in the parts. Hence modern architects have no need of the discipline of bilateral or axial symmetry to achieve aesthetic order.

Dans la plupart des cas, l'architecte doit satisfaire de nombreuses fonctions variables se référant de manières diverses les unes aux autres à l'interieur d'une structure qui doit être aussi régulière que possible grâce à l'utilisation d'éléments de nature analogue.

Une tendance à la régularité absolue signifie aussi une tendance à la monotonie, ce que l'on a peut-être déjà remarqué à l'exemple de la tour dans la ville. Le principe de la régularité modulaire renvoie davantage à une manière d'ordonner et à un moyen de donner une forme définie à un projet architectonique, qu'à un objectif définitif indépendant en soi. Car en fin de compte, la régularité est soumise aux mêmes nécessités que toute composition esthétique de revêtir une certaine mesure appropriée de signification. Et de quoi se compose cette mesure de signification n'est théoriquement pas définissable.

Dans les divers styles du passé, l'architecture s'est davantage soumise au principe de la symétrie axiale qu'à celui de la régularité tel que nous le comprenons. La signification grècque de la symétrie, «la juste proportion des divers éléments les uns envers les autres» concorde presque parfaitement avec cette signification particulière de la régularité. Cependant, la symétrie grècque sous-entendait en général que la construction était non seulement symétrique mais aussi régulière. La symétrie axiale était généralement utilisée, comme dans l'architecture baroque, dans le but d'établir de l'ordre dans l'irrégularité et de maîtriser et de relier entre eux la confusion d'éléments composants indépendants les uns des autres et les détails richement élaborés. La mise en place d'une standardisation moderne a pour effet automatique que l'on obtienne un haut niveau d'harmonie entre les divers éléments. C'est pourquoi les architectes modernes n'ont pas besoin de la discipline de la symétrie simple ni de la symétrie axiale pour atteindre un ordre esthétique.

Heute sind asymmetrische Entwurfsordnungen sowohl aus ästhetischen als auch aus technischen Gründen zu bevorzugen. Denn Asymmetrie steigert mit Sicherheit die allgemeine Attraktivität der baulichen Komposition. Und die Funktion drückt sich bei den meisten zeitgenössischen Bautypen deutlicher in asymmetrischen Formen aus.

Ein Kennzeichen für schlechte moderne Architektur ist die eigensinnige Betonung der Asymmetrie aus dekorativen Gründen. Dies kann in der Mehrzahl der Fälle nur auf Kosten von allgemeinem Konsens und gesundem Menschenverstand geschehen. Ein Kennzeichen von guter moderner Architektur hingegen ist, daß die Regelmäßigkeit der Formen sich der Spiegelsymmetrie annähert. Gelegentlich erreicht sie diese auch tatsächlich. Reine Spiegelgleichheit oder Axialsymmetrie jedoch ist eher charakteristisch für Architekten, die neu zum heutigen Stil übergewechselt sind. Sie neigen dazu, Merkmale der traditionellen Ordnung als unumstößlich zu betrachten — und indem sie daran festhalten, zeigen sie, daß sie die selbstverständlichen Folgerungen aus der neuen Ordnung der modularen Regelmäßigkeit, die die alte Ordnung ersetzt hat, nicht richtig verstanden haben.

Auf dem Gebiet der Proportionen und der Anwendung des Prinzips der Regelmäßigkeit unterscheiden sich moderne Architekten am deutlichsten voneinander. Einige bemühen sich, alle Elemente ihrer Architektur in eine einzige klare Form einzubinden und so die körperliche Einheit eines Bauwerks bis zum äußersten zu betonen. Andere bevorzugen eine offenere Architektursprache mit stärkerer Hervorhebung der organischen Beziehungen zwischen den Teilen. Die Architekten unterscheiden sich auch stark bei der Behandlung jener Teile eines Gebäudes (z. B. eines Windschutzes auf einer Dachterrasse), mit denen funktionale Erfordernisse sehr einfach befriedigt werden können. Oft sind solche charakteristischen Teile ganz von der Konstruktion des Gebäudes unabhängig und haben nur sich selbst zu tragen.

Asymmetrical schemes of design are actually preferable aesthetically as well as technically. For asymmetry certainly heightens the general interest of the composition. Function in most types of contemporary building is more directly expressed in asymmetrical form.

The mark of the bad modern architect is the positive cultivation of asymmetry for decorative reasons. For that can only be done in the majority of cases at the expense of common consistency and common sense. The mark of the good modern architect, on the other hand, is that the regularity of his designs approaches bilateral symmetry. Occasionally, indeed, he even reaches it. Bilateral or axial symmetry is, however, more usually the mark of the architect newly converted to the contemporary style. Such men tend to retain it as an irrevocable traditional discipline, failing to apprehend the full implication of the new discipline of regularity which has replaced it.

It is in the field of proportions and in the applications of the principle of regularity that modern architects differ most from one another. Some strive to arrange all the elements of their design within a single bounding shape, thus emphasizing to the utmost the unity of volume of the given building. Others prefer a more extended articulation with more emphasis on the organic relation between the parts. Architects differ greatly also in their handling of those parts of a building where, as in a wind shelter on a roof, the needs of function are very easily satisfied. Often such features are entirely unconnected with the general structure of the building and have only themselves to support.

De nos jours, il faut favoriser les ordres asymétriques en projet, aussi bien pour des raisons esthétiques que techniques. Car il est certain que l'asymétrie augmente le caractère attrayant général de la composition architectonique. Et la fonction s'exprime plus clairement, dans la plupart des types de construction contemporains, par le biais des formes asymétriques.

L'accentuation arbitraire de l'asymétrie pour des raisons décoratives constitue une caractéristique permettant de reconnaître la mauvaise architecture moderne. Ceci ne peut être réalisé, dans la plupart des cas, qu'au détriment d'un consensus général et du bon sens humain. En revanche, la bonne architecture moderne se caractérise par le fait que la régularité des formes se rapproche de la symétrie. Occasionnellement, cette dernière est effectivement réalisée. Toutefois, la symétrie pure ou axiale constitue davantage une caractéristique des architectes qui se sont récemment ralliés au style contemporain. Ils tendent à considérer les éléments distinctifs de l'ordre traditionnel comme inébranlables — et en s'y raccrochant, ils montrent qu'ils n'ont pas vraiment compris les conséquences naturelles du nouvel ordre de la régularité modulaire qui a remplacé l'ancien ordre.

C'est dans le domaine des proportions et de l'utilisation du principe de la régularité que les architectes modernes se distinguent le plus nettement les uns des autres. Certains s'efforcent d'intégrer tous les éléments de leur architecture dans une forme unique et claire et ainsi d'accentuer à l'extrême l'unité physique d'un bâtiment. D'autres préfèrent un langage architectonique plus ouvert avec une mise en valeur des rapports organiques entre les éléments. Les architectes se distinguent aussi fortement au niveau du traitement des éléments d'un bâtiment (par exemple d'un paravent sur un toit en terrasse) permettant très facilement de satisfaire aux nécessités fonctionnelles. Souvent, de tels éléments caractéristiques sont tout à fait indépendants de la construction du bâtiment et n'ont que soi-même à supporter.

Das Prinzip der Regelmäßigkeit führt nicht zu einer eindeutigen Lösung eines solchen Anpassungsproblems von Funktion an Konstruktion, da beide gleich anpassungsfähig sind. Für den Architekten, der nur den Regeln zu folgen trachtet, oder für den Funktionalisten, der an ästhetischer Kreativität nicht interessiert ist, ist es am sichersten, etwas Unauffälliges zu machen. Für den großen Architekten aber ergibt sich hier eine Möglichkeit des persönlichen Ausdrucks. Zeitweilig kann aber für den Architekten, der seiner selbst ganz sicher ist und dessen Instinkt vom Geist der ästhetischen Prinzipien des neuen Stils durchdrungen ist, diese persönliche Ausdruckssuche noch weiter führen. Sie kann, als positive Kraft, die einschränkende Disziplin der Regelmäßigkeit modifizieren, indem sie die Notwendigkeiten von Funktion und Konstruktion einander anpaßt, ohne mit dem Geist des Grundprinzips zu brechen. Bedingung für die Existenz eines wirklichen Stils und Voraussetzung für ein durchgängig hohes Niveau der Architektur ist eine strenge ästhetische Ordnung; aber das Privileg des genialen Architekten ist es, diese Ordnung zu interpretieren und sie sogar hier und da aufzugeben. Die Funktionalisten können einer solchen Auffassung nicht beipflichten. Ihr Regelwerk kennt keine ästhetischen Ziele, und sie protestieren vehement gerade gegen diese Art von persönlichem Ausdruck. Bis zu einem gewissen Punkt haben sie recht. Vernünftige Gebäude mit langweiligem Design sind besser als Architekturmonumente, deren offensichtliche gestalterische Brillanz auf Kosten von Funktion und Konstruktion geht. Aber wenn Architektur noch Kunst sein soll, dann müssen große Architekten die Freiheit haben, neue Wege der Architektur zu beschreiten.

Diese Entwicklung der ästhetischen Möglichkeiten des heutigen Stils wird in der Verwendung runder und schräger Formen in Grundrissen und Ansichten deutlich.

The principle of regularity does not lead to an exact solution of such a problem in adjusting function to structure, since both are too readily adaptable. For the architect who seeks only to follow the rules, or for the functionalist who has no positive interest in aesthetic creation, it is safest to do that which will be least startling. But for the great architect there is the opportunity for personal lyric expression.

At times, indeed, for the architect who is quite sure of himself and who is instinctively permeated with the spirit of the aesthetic disciplines of the contemporary style, this individual lyricism may go further. It may modify, as a positive force, the restricting discipline of regulartiy, composing and adjusting the necessities of function and structure without breaking with the spirit of the principle. It is the condition of the existence of a true style, the price of an architecture generally high in level, that aesthetic disciplines should be rigid, but it is the privilege of genius to interpret these disciplines, even here and there to discard them altogether. The functionalists cannot admit such a conception. Their disciplines are not in intention aesthetic and they protest most vehemently against just this sort of lyricism and personal expression. Up to a certain point they are right. Sound buildings of dull design are better than monuments of architecture whose apparent brilliance of design is paid for by inadequate provision for function and by distortion of structure. But if architecture is still to be an art, great architects must be free to go forth upon new paths of design.

This development of the aesthetic possibilities of the contemporary style is well illustrated in the use of oblique and rounded forms in plan and elevation.

Le principe de la régularité ne conduit pas à la solution sans équivoque d'un tel problème d'adaptation entre la fonction et la construction, étant donné que toutes les deux sont aussi adaptables l'une que l'autre. Pour l'architecte, qui ne vise qu'à respecter les règles, ou pour le fonctionnaliste qui ne s'intéresse pas à la créativité esthétique, le plus sûr est de faire quelque chose de discret. Mais pour le grand architecte, il trouve ici la possibilité de donner libre cours à son expression personnelle.

Parfois cependant, pour l'architecte très sûr de lui et dont l'instinct est empreint de l'esprit des principes esthétiques du nouveau style, cette recherche d'expression personnelle peut mener beaucoup plus loin. Cette recherche peut en effet, en tant que force positive, modifier la discipline restreignante de la régularité, dans la mesure où elle fait concorder les nécessités de la fonction et de la construction sans rompre avec l'esprit du principe fondamental. La condition de l'existence d'un style véritable et de la naissance d'une architecture au niveau continuellement élevé réside dans un sévère ordre esthétique; mais le privilège de l'architecte génial consiste dans sa capacité d'interpréter cet ordre et même de l'abandonner ici ou là. Les fonctionnalistes ne peuvent pas se rallier à une telle conception. Leur œuvre type ne connaît pas d'objectifs esthétiques et c'est justement contre ce type d'expression personnelle qu'ils protestent avec véhémence. Jusqu'à un certain point, ils ont raison. Les bâtiments raisonnables avec un design ennuyeux valent mieux que les monuments d'architecture dont la composition manifestement brillante s'accomplit au détriment de la fonction et de la construction. Mais si l'architecture doit encore être considérée comme de l'art, les grands architectes doivent avoir la liberté d'emprunter de nouvelles voies de l'architecture.

Ce développement des possibilités esthétiques du style contemporain se fait nettement jour dans l'utilisation de formes rondes et obliques dans les coupes et façades.

Derartige Abweichungen von der grundsätzlichen Rechtwinkligkeit sind nur gelegentlich durch die Funktion bedingt, und sie können das gleichmäßige Raster des Tragskeletts verkomplizieren. Sie brechen eindeutig mit der strengen Regelmäßigkeit.
Nicht-rechtwinklige Formen führen besonders dann, wenn sie selten vorkommen, ein ästhetisches Element von außerordentlicher Anziehungskraft ein. Der Architekt mit Mut wendet sich von Zeit zu Zeit diesen Formen zu; erkennt, daß er sie, gebändigt durch seine Einfühlungsgabe und im deutlichen Gegensatz zur Ordnung der modularen Regelmäßigkeit, verwenden muß. Rundungen werden bei Alltagsarchitektur selten gebraucht, aber bei bedeutenden Gebäuden, bei denen sich der Architekt zur Suche nach einem starken eigenen Ausdruck berechtigt fühlt, werden sie zu den ästhetischen Komponenten gehören, die am stärksten positiv oder negativ bewertet werden. Runde und schräge Formen taugen selten zur billigsten Lösung eines gegebenen Problems. Aber wenn man sie sich leisten kann, triumphieren oder scheitern sie allein auf ästhetischem Gebiet.
Die Funktionalisten und alle, die zu ängstlich sind, die strenge Regelmäßigkeit zu durchbrechen, geraten leicht in die Gefahr der Wiederholung stilistischer Gemeinplätze. Reihen von gleich großen Fenstern in regelmäßiger Verteilung und Fassaden, bei denen Glasbänder sich mit Putzbändern abwechseln, nur unterbrochen durch gelegentliche Treppenhausfenster, sind in Europa schon verbreitet genug und haben ihre Anziehungskraft längst verloren. Auch die strengsten Verteidiger des Internationalen Stils müssen zugeben, daß die zu rigide Anwendung des Prinzips der Regelmäßigkeit und die phantasielose Wiederholung der gebräuchlichsten Kompositionsschemata zu vielen stumpfsinnigen Gebäuden geführt haben. Aber derartige Gebäude sind trotzdem den Bauten jener sorglosen modernen Architekten vorzuziehen, die nicht einmal die Existenz eines Prinzips der Regelmäßigkeit begreifen können.

Such exceptions to general rectangularity are only occasionally demanded by function and they may introduce complications in the regular skeleton of the structure. They are, of course, a definite breach of rigid regularity.
Non-rectangular shapes, particularly if they occur infrequently, introduce an aesthetic element of the highest positive interest. To them the architect of courage turns from time to time, realizing that he must employ them chiefly with the sanctions of genius and in definite opposition to the discipline of regulartiy. They need seldom occur in ordinary building, but in monuments where the architect feels justified in seeking for a strongly personal expression, curves will be among the elements which give most surely extreme positive or negative aesthetic value.
Curved and oblique forms seldom find a place in the cheapest solution of a given problem. But if they can be afforded, they succeed, as they fail, on aesthetic grounds alone.
The functionalists, and those who are too timid to break with rigid regularity, fall rather into the aesthetic danger of repeating the commonplaces of the style. Ranges of equal-sized windows, set in an unbroken pattern, façades where ribbon of glass alternates with ribbon of stucco, broken only by an occasional stair window, are already frequent enough in Europe to have lost the interest of mere novelty. The most determined defender of the international style must admit that the too rigid application of the principle of regularity, the unimaginative repetition of the most obvious schemes of composition, has produced much very dull building. But such work is nevertheless preferable to the building of the careless modern architects who have failed even to apprehend the existence of a principle of regularity.

De telles déviations par rapport aux formes fondamentales à angle droit ne sont qu'occasionnellement dues aux besoins de la fonction, et elles peuvent compliquer la grille régulière du squelette porteur. Elles brisent sans aucun doute une sévère régularité.
Particulièrement lorsqu'elles font rarement apparition, les formes sans angles droits introduisent un élément au charme extraordinaire. L'architecte courageux s'y consacrera de temps en temps; il reconnaît qu'il doit les utiliser, maîtrisées par son don d'intuition et en contraste net par rapport à l'ordre de la régularité modulaire. Les arrondis sont rarement utilisés dans l'architecture quotidienne, mais dans les bâtiments importants, où l'architecte se sent confirmé dans sa recherche d'une expression propre et forte, ils feront partie des composantes esthétiques qui seront le plus jugées positivement ou négativement. Les formes rondes et obliques font rarement affaire lorsque l'on cherche la solution la moins chère à un problème. Mais quand on peut se le permettre, elles triomphent ou représentent une défaite, uniquement dans le domaine esthétique.
Les fonctionnalistes et tous ceux qui sont trop craintifs pour faire éclater cette sévère régularité, se trouvent rapidement en danger de paraphraser des lieux communs stylistiques. Les rangées de fenêtres de même taille en répartition régulière et sur des façades où les bandes de verre et des bandes de crépi se succèdent en alternance, seulement interrompues par d'occasionnelles fenêtres de montées d'escaliers, sont déjà assez répandues en Europe et ont perdu de leur charme depuis longtemps. De plus, les défenseurs les plus acharnés du Style International sont bien obligés de reconnaître qu'une utilisation trop rigide du principe de la régularité et la répétition sans fantaisie des schémas de composition les plus usuels ont conduit à la construction de nombreux bâtiments stupides. Mais de tels bâtiments sont malgré tout préférables aux constructions de ces architectes modernes dépourvus de scrupules et incapables même de concevoir l'existence d'un principe de régularité.

Jene, die dem neuen Stil zu folgen suchen, ohne ihn zu verstehen, produzieren Bauten, die nicht nur langweilig, sondern auch ärgerlich sind. Sie mißbrauchen Eckfenster; sie schaffen es nicht, sichtbare Giebel und Satteldächer zu vermeiden; Steinblöcke schichten sie aufeinander, als ob sie noch mitten in der massiven Architektur der Vergangenheit steckten. Beim Gestalten von Fassaden arrangieren sie die Elemente zu einer auffällig gewollten Asymmetrie, und ihre Anordnung der Fenster folgt keinem erkennbaren technischen oder ästhetischen Ordnungsprinzip. Für sie ist der neue Stil, den sie parodieren, einfach Architektur der Semimoderne ohne Dekoration, ein erbärmliches Produkt, das sie als Individualismus rechtfertigen. Die amerikanischen Funktionalisten gehören zu dieser Sorte, obwohl sie sich nicht so sehr dem Parodieren der Erscheinungsformen des neuen Stils widmen. Wo sie ihre Langweiligkeit nicht aus Rücksicht auf die ästhetischen Wünsche ihrer Bauherren hinter billiger Kosmetik verbergen, bevorzugen sie eine Anordnung der Fenster in vertikalen Bändern. Dies führt zu einem historisierenden Strebepfeilereffekt ohne jede Beziehung zu den modernen Methoden der Skelettbauweise. Die dadurch entstehende Vertikalgliederung wird in Amerika noch immer bewundert, hauptsächlich, weil sie das aufwärtsstrebende Bild der gotischen Türme der Vergangenheit in Erinnerung ruft. Sogar bei Bauten mit dominierender Horizontalität in der Fensteranordnung werden Gruppen von Strebepfeilern in der Mitte oder an den Ecken der Gebäude als Konzession an den Auftraggeber hinzugefügt. Horizontalität, das auffallendste Merkmal des Internationalen Stils, was seine visuelle Wirkung betrifft, wird vom durchschnittlichen amerikanischen Bauherrn noch immer nicht akzeptiert. Nur große Künstler sind fähig, mit begrenzten Mitteln großartige Wirkungen zu erzielen. Architekten bilden da keine Ausnahme. Aber es ist das Privileg großer Architekten, die ästhetische Ordnung des Stils in Übereinstimmung mit ihrem Geist zu interpretieren, anstatt genauen Festlegungen zu folgen.

Those who try to follow the new style without understanding it produce work which is not only dull but irritating. They abuse corner windows; they fail to avoid the visibly gabled roof; they pile up blocks as if they were still dealing with the massive architecture of the past. In designing façades they dispose the elements with an obvious and gratuitous asymmetry and they arrange their fenestration according to no discoverable principle of order, aesthetic or technical. For them the new style that they parody is merely the architecture of the half-moderns with the decoration omitted, a makeshift product of apologetic individualism.
The American functionalists are of this order although they are less given to parodying the surface of the new style. Where they do not hide their dullness under cheap cosmetics in deference to the aesthetic desires of the client, they prefer rather to group their windows in vertical bands. This gives a traditional buttress effect quite without relation to modern methods of steel cage construction. The resultant verticality of design is still admired in America, chiefly because it recalls the aspiring quality of the Gothic towers of the past. Even in buildings with predominantly horizontal window arrangement, groups of buttresses in the center or at the corners of the building are added as a concession to the client. For horizontality, which is the most conspicuous characteristic of the international style as judged in terms of effect, is still unacceptable aesthetically to the average American client.
Only great artists are capable of achieving brilliant effects with the limited means. Architects are no exception. But it is the privilege of great architects to interpret the aesthetic discipline of the style according to the spirit rather than the letter.

Ceux qui tentent de respecter le nouveau style sans le comprendre produisent des constructions qui ne sont pas seulement ennuyeuses, mais aussi fâcheuses. Ils malmènent les fenêtres d'angle; ils ne parviennent pas à éviter les pignons visibles et les toits à bâtière; ils empilent les blocs de pierre les uns sur les autres, comme s'ils se trouvaient encore au cœur de l'architecture massive du passé. Dans la composition des façades, ils arrangent les éléments en une asymétrie voyante et voulue, et leur ordre des fenêtres ne suit aucun principe d'ordre technique ou esthétique reconnaissable. Pour eux, le nouveau style qu'ils parodient est simplement l'architecture du semi-moderne sans décoration, un lamentable produit qu'ils justifient par leur individualisme. Les fonctionnalistes américains font partie de cette catégorie, bien qu'ils ne se consacrent pas tellement à la parodie des formes d'apparition du nouveau style. Là où ils ne dissimulent pas leur ennui sous une couche cosmétique par égards pour les souhaits de leur commettants, ils préfèrent un arrangement des fenêtres en bandes verticales. Ceci conduit à un effet historicisant de contrefort dénué de tout rapport avec les méthodes modernes du mode de construction à squelette. L'articulation verticale en découlant est toujours admirée en Amérique, notamment parce qu'elle évoque l'image de l'aspiration vers le haut des tours gothiques du passé. Même dans les constructions où l'ordre des fenêtres est à dominante horizontale, on ajoute des groupes de contreforts au milieu ou aux angles du bâtiments pour céder aux désirs du commettant. L'horizontalité, la caractéristique la plus marquante du Style International, en ce qui concerne son effet visuel, n'est toujours pas acceptée par le maître d'ordre américain moyen.
Seuls les grands artistes sont capables d'atteindre des effets exceptionnels avec des moyens réduits. Les architectes ne constituent là aucune exception. Mais c'est le privilège des grands architectes que d'interpréter l'ordre esthétique du style en harmonie avec leur esprit, au lieu de suivre de précises prescriptions.

Wer den Regeln folgt, wer die Forderungen einer Architektur akzeptiert, die nicht Masse ist, sondern umschlossener Raum, wer mit dem Prinzip der Regelmäßigkeit übereinstimmt, kann Gebäude schaffen, die wenigstens ästhetisch in Ordnung sind. Wenn diese Prinzipien eher negativ als positiv erscheinen, dann weil die Architektur in den letzten anderthalb Jahrhunderten hauptsächlich darunter zu leiden hatte, daß all jene, die sich Architekten nannten, die Freiheiten des Genies für sich in Anspruch nahmen.

Es wäre besser, die Welt würde nur noch in Übereinstimmung mit den rigiden anti-ästhetischen Theorien der extremen europäischen Funktionalisten bauen, als wenn die Ausschweifungen der Architektur des 19. Jahrhunderts andauerten. Die Individualisten am Beginn des 20. Jahrhunderts reagierten auf diese Ausschweifungen mit der Extravaganz ihrer Ornamente. Aber ihre Reaktion schuf keine festen Regeln. Sie hatten weder gemeinsame Ziele, noch waren sie ihren Ergebnissen gegenüber kritisch genug. Die Ornamentik der Semimodernen hat den Test zeitlicher Gültigkeit nicht bestanden, genausowenig wie diejenige der kultivierteren Neohistoristen. Die Weiterverwendung dieser oberflächlich neuartigen Dekorationen, die die Semimodernen so wirkungsvoll hervorbrachten, unterscheidet die Mehrzahl der amerikanischen modernen Architekten von denjenigen in Europa.

Ein drittes Prinzip: Vermeidung aufgesetzter Dekorationen

Das Fehlen von Ornamenten hilft ebenso wie regelhafte Horizontalität, den gegenwärtigen Stil von den Stilen der Vergangenheit und deren verschiedenen Abarten der letzten anderthalb Jahrhunderte oberflächlich zu unterscheiden. Aufgesetzte Ornamente mögen für die Architektur der Vergangenheit bedeutsam oder nicht wichtig gewesen sein, aber sie waren mit Sicherheit vorhanden. Es wäre zu einfach, auf der Ansicht zu beharren, daß die besten Bauten seit 1800 diejenigen mit den wenigsten Ornamenten seien.

Anyone who follows the rules, who accepts the implications of an architecture that is not mass but volume, and who conforms to the principle of regularity can produce buildings which are at least aesthetically sound. If these principles seem more negative than positive, it is because architecture has suffered chiefly in the last century and a half from the extension of the sanctions of genius to all who have called themselves architects.

It were better that the world build only according to the rigid anti-aesthetic theories of the extreme European functionalists than that nineteenth century debauchery of design should continue. The individualists of the early twentieth century reacted against that debauchery with its extravagance of applied ornament. But their reaction created no fixed standards. They were neither consistent in their aims nor critical enough of the results. The ornament of the half-moderns has failed to stand the test of time even as well as that of the more cultured revivalists. The continuance of this superficially novel decoration which the half-moderns orginated most effectually distinguishes the mass of American modern architecture from that of Europe.

A third principle: The avoidance of applied decoration

Absence of ornament as much as regular horizontality to differentiate superficially the current style from the styles of the past and from the various manners of the last century and a half. Applied ornament may not have been significant or important in the architecture of the past, but it certainly existed. It is easier to defend the claim that the finest buildings built since 1800 were those least ornamented.

Quiconque suit les règles, quiconque accepte les exigences d'une architecture qui n'est pas masse mais espace compris dans une enveloppe, quiconque est d'accord avec le principe de la régularité, peut créer des bâtiments qui sont au moins corrects sur le plan esthétique. Sie ces principes paraissent plutôt négatifs que positifs, c'est parce que l'architecture, au cours des cent cinquante années passés, a dû souffrir du fait que tous ceux qui se prétendaient architectes ont revendiqué pour eux les libertés du génie. Il vaudrait mieux que le monde ne construise plus qu'en harmonie avec les rigides théories anti-esthétiques des extrêmes fonctionnalistes européens plutôt que les débordements de l'architecture du XIXe siècle ne se perpétuent. Les individualistes, au début du XXe siècle, ont répondu à ces débordements par l'extravagance de leurs ornements. Mais leur réaction n'a donné jour à aucune règle fixe. Ils ne possédaient pas d'objectifs communs ni ne considéraient leurs résultats avec assez d'esprit critique. Le style des ornements des semimodernes n'a pas réussi le test de validité temporelle, aussi peu que celui des néohistoristes cultivés. La réutilisation de ces décorations superficiellement nouvelles que les semi-modernes ont inaugurées avec tant d'effet, permet de distinguer la plupart des architectes modernes américains des européens.

Un troisième principe: L'absence de décorations appliquées

L'absence d'ornements, tout autant que la règle de l'horizontale, aide à différencier superficiellement le style actuel des styles du passé et des dérivés de ces styles apparus pendant le dernier siècle et demi. Que les ornements appliqués aient été d'importance ou non pour l'architecture du passé, ce qui est sûr, c'est qu'ils étaient présents. Il serait trop facile de s'obstiner dans l'opinion que les meilleures bâtiments construits depuis 1800 sont ceux qui présentent le moins d'ornements.

Das Versagen des neuen Historismus lag vielleicht sowohl an der Unfähigkeit, die Bedingungen für eine handwerkliche Arbeit wiederherzustellen, die einst dem baulichen Ornament seine Gültigkeit verlieh, als auch an der Unmöglichkeit, den Geist der alten Stile modernen Baumethoden anzupassen.

Es wäre lächerlich, kategorisch zu behaupten, daß es mit dem baulichen Ornament in der Architektur vorbei ist. Nichtsdestoweniger muß man sich über etwas im klaren sein: Die Bedingungen für die Schaffung von Ornamenten sind heute noch ungünstiger als während des letzten Jahrhunderts. Seit der Mitte des 18. Jahrhunderts hat die Ausführungsqualität der Ornamente stetig abgenommen. Sogar die während der Neogotik geförderte Wiederbelebung der Handwerkskunst konnte am Lauf der Dinge nichts ändern. Im ganzen gesehen, hat jede Traditionalistengeneration in dieser Hinsicht schlechtere Bedingungen als die jeweils vorangehende vorgefunden.

Es gab jedoch nie Architektur ohne irgendwelche Dekorationselemente. Denn Dekoration kann als etwas betrachtet werden, was nicht nur bauliche Ornamentik umfaßt, sondern alle möglichen Komponenten der Gestaltung, die dem Ganzen Reiz und Vielfalt verleihen. Das architektonische Detail, das in der modernen Baukonstruktion genau wie in der Vergangenheit gebraucht wird, sorgt in der zeitgenössischen Architektur für eine gewisse Ausschmückung. Tatsächlich sorgte das Detail, wie es heute durch die Baukonstruktion bedingt ist oder diese veranschaulicht, auch bei den reinen Stilen der Vergangenheit für die meisten der dekorativen Elemente. Die Tatsache, daß es heute so wenige verschiedene Details gibt, steigert die dekorative Wirkung derer, die vorhanden sind. Ihre formale Ordnung ist eines der wichtigsten Mittel, Ausgewogenheit zwischen den Teilen eines Entwurfs zu erreichen.

Die Handhabung von freistehenden Stützen ist – wie diejenige von Dachabschlüssen – eher ein Nebenproblem als eine fundamentale Frage. Die besten Architekten haben allerdings hier die gleiche Finesse gezeigt wie die griechischen und römischen Baumeister.

The failure of revivalism probably lay quite as much in the inability to recreate the conditions of craftsmanship which once made applied ornament aesthetically valid, as in the impossibility of adapting the spirit of old styles to new methods of construction.

It would be ridiculous to state categorically that there will never be successful applied ornament in architecture again. It is nevertheless clear that conditions are today even less propitious for the production of ornament than they were during the last century. Since the middle of the eighteenth century the quality of the execution of ornament has steadily declined. Even the renaissance of craftsmanship sponsored by the Mediaevalists failed to turn the tide. On the whole each generation of traditionalists has been worse served in this respect than its predecessor.

Architecture, however, has never been without other elements of decoration. For decoration may be considered to include not only applied ornament, but all the incidental features of design which give interest and variety to the whole. Architectural detail, which is required as much by modern structure as by the structure of the past, provides the decoration of contemporary architecture. Indeed, detail actually required by structure or symbolic of the underlying structure provided most of the decoration of the purer styles of the past.

The fact that there is so little detail today increases the decorative effect of what there is. Its ordering is one of the chief means by which consistency is achieved in the parts of a design.

The handling of isolated supports like the handling of wall capping is incidental rather than fundamental. The best architects, however, have shown in this a finesse equal to that of the Greek and Gothic builders.

La déchéance du nouvel historisme a peut-être été aussi bien causée par l'incapacité de reproduire les conditions nécessaires à un travail artisanal ayant permis autrefois d'octroyer sa validité à l'ornement architectonique que par l'impossibilité d'adapter l'esprit des anciens styles aux méthodes de construction modernes.

Il serait ridicule de prétendre catégoriquement que le temps de l'ornement architectonique est révolu. Néanmoins, il est nécessaire d'avoir conscience du fait suivant: les conditions de la création d'ornements sont encore moins favorables qu'au siècle dernier. Depuis le milieu du XVIIIe siècle, la qualité de réalisation des ornements n'a cessé de sombrer. Même la reprise de l'artisanat d'art encouragé pendant l'époque néogothique n'a rien pu changer au cours des choses. Vu dans l'ensemble, chaque génération de traditionnalistes a trouvé, sous cet angle, de moins bonnes conditions que celles dont avait pu jouir la génération qui l'avait précédée.

Toutefois, il n'y a jamais eu d'architecture sans de quelconques éléments de décoration. Car la décoration peut être considérée comme quelque chose ne contenant pas seulement l'ensemble des ornements de la construction, mais aussi toutes sortes de composantes de la création qui octroient charme et diversité au tout. Le détail architectonique que l'on utilise dans la construction de bâtiment moderne comme dans le passé, remplit, dans l'architecture contemporaine, une fonction décorative. En effet, le détail représentait, comme ceci est dépendant aujourd'hui de la construction du bâtiment ou comme celle-ci le met en évidence, la plupart des éléments décoratifs dans les styles purs du passé également. Le fait qu'il existe de nos jours si peu de détails différents augmente l'effet de ceux qui sont présents. Leur ordre formel constitue l'un des moyens les plus importants pour atteindre un équilibre harmonieux entre les divers éléments d'un projet.

L'utilisation de colonnes détachées est – comme celles des bords de toits – plutôt un problème secondaire qu'une question fondamentale. Les meilleurs architectes ont d'ailleurs fait ici preuve de la même finesse que les maîtres d'œuvre grecs et romains.

Wo freistehende Stützen in geschlossene Baukörper übergehen, betonen die meisten Architekten den Bezug der Stützen zum Tragskelett der darüberliegenden Konstruktion und nicht zu der umhüllenden Fassadenfläche. In Stahlbetonausführung sind runde Querschnitte ästhetisch – und gewöhnlich auch technisch – am besten, weil sie sich visuell stark von der Fassadenfläche abheben. In Innenbereichen stört die runde Form in visueller und verkehrsmäßiger Hinsicht weniger als eine quadratische oder rechteckige Stütze. Wo die Brandschutzbestimmungen keine vollständige Ummantelung verlangen, wirkt die sichtbare Stahlstütze unübertrefflich leicht und elegant. Auf diese Art kann den sichtbaren Stützelementen wieder Bedeutung und Unabhängigkeit gegeben werden. Brüstungen und Geländer haben für die heutige Architektur eine gleich große Bedeutung wie Balustraden für die Architektur des 17. und 18. Jahrhunderts. In vielen Fällen wird die Brüstung als Fortführung der Außenwand behandelt, sie umschließt die Dachterrasse als Mauer, wie die Außenwände das Rauminnere im Geschoß darunter.

Die besten Architekten widmen den Details besondere Aufmerksamkeit. Obwohl Details Nebenprobleme darstellen, verlangen sie doch mehr als beiläufige Beachtung. Gute Details schmücken ein modernes Bauwerk genauso, wie es die funktionalen Säulen und Friese der klassisch-antiken und gotischen Architektur taten. Wenn es heute wirklich einen gültigen Architekturstil gibt, muß er diesen Aspekt genau so wie die wichtigeren Dinge bestimmen. Nachlässige Architekten überlassen Details dem Zufall und verderben damit gute Ansätze. Wer Architektur nur als Wissenschaft ansieht, ist gewöhnlich ein so gewissenhafter Techniker, daß er die Detailbehandlung mit Kompetenz, wenn nicht mit Brillanz beherrscht.

Where isolated supports pass up into a closed construction most architects indicate the coherence of the posts with the skeleton of the construction above and not with its covering surfaces. In ferroconcrete construction rounded forms are aesthetically, and usually technically, superior since they remain visually quite separate from the wall surface. The rounded form in interiors interferes less with vision and circulation than a square or oblong pier. Where fire laws do not require more complete insulation, the actual metal pier is exceedingly light and elegant. In this way significance and independence can be given again to visible supports.

Parapets and railings have an importance in contemporary architecture as great as that of balustrades in the architecture of the seventeenth and eighteenth centuries. In many cases the parapet is properly treated as a continuation of the wall surface, since it encloses the roof terrace just as the wall encloses the interior room space below.

The best architects give particular thought to matters of detail. Although they are incidentals, they require more than incidental attention. Fine details decorate a modern design just as did the functional columns and mouldings of Greek and Gothic architecture. If there truly be a contemporary style of architecture, it must control these as well as larger matters. Careless architects leave details to chance, thus marring creditable work. Those who claim that architecture is merely science are usually conscientious enough technologists to handle with competence, if not with brilliance, such matters of detail.

Là où des colonnes détachées se fondent dans le corps de la construction, la plupart des architectes accentuent le lien des colonnes avec le squelette porteur de la construction se trouvant au-dessus et non pas avec la surface de la façade enveloppante. Dans une version de béton armé, les coupes transversales rondes sont esthétiquement – et en général aussi techniquement – les meilleures, parce qu'elles tranchent fortement, sur le plan visuel, sur la surface de la façade. Dans le domaine intérieur, la forme ronde dérange moins sur le plan visuel et en ce qui concerne la circulation, qu'une colonne carrée ou rectangulaire. Là où les prescriptions de sécurité contre les incendies n'exigent pas de chemise de béton complète, la colonne d'acier visible produit un effet inégalable de légèreté et d'élégance. De cette manière, on peut redonner aux éléments visibles de soutien plus de signification et d'indépendance.

Dans l'architecture d'aujourd'hui, les parapets et les rampes jouent un rôle aussi important que les balustrades dans l'architecture des XVIIᵉ et XVIIIᵉ siècles. Dans beaucoup de cas, le parapet est traité comme un prolongement du mur extérieur, il entoure le toit en terrasse en qualité de mur, comme les murs extérieurs le font à l'étage du dessous, entourant l'espace intérieur.

Les meilleurs architectes consacrent une attention particulière aux détails. Bien que les détails représentent des problèmes secondaires, ils exigent pourtant plus qu'une simple considération superficielle. De bons détails décorent un bâtiment moderne de la même façon que le faisaient les colonnes et frises fonctionnelles de l'époque antique-classique et de l'architecture gothique. S'il existe aujourd'hui vraiment un style d'architecture valable, il doit déterminer cet aspect exactement comme il le fait pour les choses plus importantes. Les architectes négligeants laissent ces détails au hasard et gâchent ainsi de bonnes bases. Celui qui ne considère l'architecture que comme une science est généralement un technicien tellement consciencieux qu'il maîtrise le traitement des détails avec compétence, si ce n'est avec brillo.

Neben dem architektonischen Detail bieten passende Werke der Skulptur und Malerei die Gelegenheit, zeitgenössische Bauten angemessen zu schmücken, ohne in bloßes aufgesetztes Ornamentieren abzugleiten.

Ob aus den beiden verschiedenen Gattungen der Dekoration – architektonischem Detail und hinzugefügten Werken der Malerei und Skulptur – der heutige Stil mit der Zeit eine eigene Ornamentik entwickeln wird, kann niemand sagen. Das angeblich neue Ornament, von dem die Architektur sich gerade befreit hat, hat uns gegenüber lediglich dekorativen Innovationen wachsam gemacht. Die Aussagen aller kritisch formulierten Theorien neigen dazu, die Notwendigkeit des Ornaments als Selbstzweck zu verneinen. Einige Autoren interpretieren sogar die gesamte Ornamentik guter Architektur der Vergangenheit als nichts anders als Erweiterung freier Bildhauerei oder als Weiterführung überlieferter Details, die ursprünglich baukonstruktive Bedeutung hatten.

Der Stil unserer Zeit setzt für dekorative Elemente einen hohen, aber erreichbaren Standard: gut oder gar nicht. Das Gesetz ist eher aristokratisch als puritanisch. Es zielt sowohl darauf ab, Monstrositäten, durch die das 19. Jahrhundert so gründlich versagte, zu verhindern, als auch Meisterwerke, die das 19. Jahrhundert so wenig hervorbrachte, in ihrer Entstehung zu fördern.

Auch bei der Anwendung von Farbe ist Zurückhaltung die allgemeine Regel. In der Frühzeit des neuen Stils waren weiße Putzflächen allgegenwärtig. Zu einer Zeit, als die Architekten mit entscheidenderen Fragen beschäftig waren, wurde der Farbe nur wenig Aufmerksamkeit geschenkt. Darauf folgte eine Periode, während der die Verwendung von Farbe großen Rang erlangte. In Holland und Deutschland verwendete man kleine Flächen mit reinen Elementarfarben, in Frankreich große Felder mit gedämpfteren Farben. Die beiden Gestaltungsweisen sind großenteils dem Einfluß zweier verschiedener Schulen der abstrakten Malerei zuzuschreiben, für die die Namen von Mondrian auf der einen, von Ozenfant auf der anderen Seite stehen.

Besides architectural detail, related subordinate works of sculpture and painting have on occasion been successfully used to decorate contemporary buildings without degenerating into mere applied ornament.

Whether from these two different forms of decoration – architectural detail and related works of painting and sculpture – the contemporary style will in time develop an ornament of its own as did the styles of the past, no one can say. The supposedly novel ornament from which architecture is now freeing itself has put us on our guard against innovations which are merely decorative. The force of all self-conscious theory tends to deny the necessity for ornament on the fine architecture of the past as but an extension of free sculpture or as a continuance of inherited detail which originally had structural meaning.

The current style sets a high but not impossible standard for decoration: better none at all unless it be good. The principle is aristocratic rather than puritanical. It aims as much at making monstrosities impossible, at which the nineteenth century so signally failed, as at assuring masterpieces, at which the nineteenth century had no very extraordinary success.

Also in the use of color the genaral rule is restraint. In the earliest days of the contemporary style white stucco was ubiquitous. Little thought was given to color at a time when architects were preoccupied with more essential matters. Then followed a period when the use of color began to receive considerable attention. In Holland and Germany small areas of bright elementary colors were used; in France, large areas of more neutral color. The two practices were in large part due to the influence of two different schools of abstract painting, as represented on the one hand by Mondriaan and on the other by Ozenfant.

Outre le détail architectonique, certaines œuvres offrent à la sculpture et à la peinture l'occasion de décorer les constructions contemporaines de manière adaptée sans dériver dans le contexte de l'ornementation simplement appliquée.

Personne ne peut dire si, avec le temps, le style actuel développera son propre type d'ornements à partir de ces diverses espèces de décoration – à savoir le détail architectonique et l'ajout d'œuvres de peinture et de sculpture. L'ornement, soi-disant nouveau, dont l'architecture vient de se défaire, nous a donné l'éveil envers les innovations uniquement décoratives. Les déclarations de toutes les théories formulées de manière critique tendent à réfuter la nécessité de l'ornement au seul but décoratif. Certains auteurs interprètent même l'ensemble des ornements de la bonne architecture du passé comme rien d'autre qu'un élargissement de la sculpture libre ou comme la perpétuation de détails transmis qui possédaient à l'origine une signification dans la construction du bâtiment.

Le style de notre temps définit un standard élevé, mais accessible, pour les éléments décoratifs: bons ou absents. Cette loi est plutôt aristocratique que puritaine. Elle vise aussi bien à éviter les monstruosités à cause desquelles le XIXᵉ siècle a si profondément péché, qu'à encourager la création de chefs-d'œuvre auxquels le XIXᵉ siècle a si rarement donné naissance.

Dans l'application de la couleur également, la retenue constitue une règle générale. Au début du nouveau style, les surfaces de crépi blanc étaient partout présentes. A une époque où les architectes étaient préoccupés par des questions décisives, ils n'ont guère prêté attention à la couleur. A ceci a succédé une période pendant laquelle l'utilisation de la couleur a subitement gagné une grande importance. En Hollande et en Allemagne, on s'est mis à utiliser de petites surfaces recouvertes des couleurs élémentaires pures, en France de grandes surfaces avec des couleurs plus feutrées. Ces deux manières de décorer découlent de la peinture abstraite, l'une à la suite de Mondrian, l'autre d'Ozenfant.

In beiden Fällen wurden die Farben künstlich aufgetragen, der größte Teil der Außenfläche blieb weiß. Gegenwärtig wird Farbe seltener verwendet. Die Farben natürlicher Fassadenmaterialien und die natürlichen Töne der Metallprofile werden eindeutig bevorzugt. Wo Metall gestrichen ist, mindert eine dunkle, neutrale Tönung das optische Gewicht der Fensterrahmen. Putzflächen – weiß oder nicht – sollten, auch wenn sie eingefärbt wurden, als Naturfarben empfunden werden können. Die frühere Verwendung von reinen Farben hatte ihren Sinn in der Erregung von Aufmerksamkeit für den neuen Stil, aber sie konnte nicht lange befriedigen. Die Farben fielen bald nicht mehr auf und begannen zu langweilen; ihre rationale Präzision und Frische wirkte schnell abgeschmackt. Wenn Architektur nicht zu Plakatwänden verkommen soll, muß Farbe sowohl technisch als auch psychologisch Bestand haben.

Die natürliche Umgebung ist sowohl Gegensatz als auch Hintergrund, der die künstlichen, von Architekten geschaffenen Qualitäten zur Geltung bringt. Die Wahl des Bauplatzes und die Anordnung der Gebäude auf dem Grundstück sind die wichtigsten Anliegen des Internationalen Stils in bezug auf die natürliche Umgebung. Die ursprünglichen Schönheiten des Baugeländes sollten soweit wie möglich erhalten werden. Offene Außenräume allein reichen nicht aus; etwas von der Zwanglosigkeit und dem Reiz der unberührten Natur sollte ebenfalls spürbar sein. Terrassen können das Haus nach außen erweitern, aber jenseits der Terrasse sollte eindeutig die Herrschaft der Natur beginnen. Der formal durchgestaltete Garten hat in Verbindung mit dem Internationalen Stil keine Daseinsberechtigung. Eine aus der Architektur abgeleitete Ästhetik des rechten Winkels kann nicht auf die Landschaftsgestaltung übertragen werden, ohne den beruhigenden Gegensatz zum natürlichen Hintergrund teilweise einzubüßen.

In both cases colors were artifically applied and the majority of wall surfaces remained white.

At present applied color is used less. The color of natural surfacing materials and the natural metal color of detail is definitely preferred. Where the metal is painted, a dark neutral tone minimizes the apparent weight of the window frame. In surfaces of stucco, white or off-white, even where it is obtained with paint, is felt to constitute the natural color. The earlier use of bright color had value in attracting attention to the new style, but it could not long remain pleasing. It ceased to startle and began to bore; its mechanical sharpness and freshness became rapidly tawdry. If architecture is not to resemble billboards, color should be both technically and psychologically permanent.

Natural surroundings are at once a contrast and a background emphasizing the artifical values created by architects. Choice of site, and the arrangement of buildings upon the site: these are the prime problems of the international style in relation to natural surroundings. As far as possible the original beauties of the site should be preserved. Mere open spaces are not enough for repose; something of the ease and grace of untouched nature is needed as well. Terraces may extend the house outside its own boundaries, but beyond the terraces the reign of nature should clearly begin. The elaborate formal garden has no place in connection with the international style. An aesthetic of right angles derived from architecture cannot be generally applied to landscape design without diminishing the reposeful contrast of the natural background. Additional planting needed for protection or shelter, however, should usually keep to straight lines and avoid the imitation of natural irregularity. Roads and paths should be laid out for efficient communication, not with picturesque curves.

Dans les deux cas, on appliquait les couleurs artificiellement, la plus grande partie de la surface extérieure demeurait blanche.

Actuellement, on utilise moins souvent la couleur. On donne nettement la préférence aux couleurs des matériaux naturels des façades et aux tons naturels des profils métalliques. Là où le métal a été peint, un coloris sombre et naturel estompe l'importance optique des cadres des fenêtres. Les surfaces de crépi – blanches ou non – sont censées, même si elles ont été teintées, être ressenties comme naturelles. Le sens de l'ancienne utilisation de couleurs pures était d'attirer l'attention sur le nouveau style, mais elle n'a pas pu satisfaire pendant longtemps. Les couleurs ont bientôt cessé d'attirer l'attention et ont commencé à ennuyer; leur précision et leur fraîcheur rationnelles n'ont pas tardé à lasser. Si l'on ne veut pas que l'architecture tourne en murs pour affichage, la couleur doit avoir une tenue aussi bien technique que psychologique.

L'environnement naturel fournit aussi bien un contraste qu'un arrière-plan permettant de mettre en valeur les qualités créées artificiellement par les architectes. Le choix de l'emplacement de la construction et l'ordre des bâtiments sur le terrain sont les points d'intérêt les plus importants du Style International en ce qui concerne l'environnement naturel. Dans la mesure du possible, les beautés d'origine du terrain de construction doivent être conservées. Les espaces extérieurs ouverts ne suffisent pas à eux seuls; il est également souhaitable que l'on sente encore un peu de cette absence de contraintes et de l'attrait de la nature sauvage.

Les terrasses peuvent élargir la maison vers l'extérieur, mais au-delà des terrasses, il faut que le règne de la nature commence manifestement. Le jardin formellement arrangé ne possède aucune justification d'exister en relation avec le Style International. Il n'est pas possible de projeter cette esthétique de l'ange droit dérivée de l'architecture sur la composition du paysage sans détruire en partie ce contraste si appaisant fourni par l'arrière-plan naturel.

A R G E N T I N I E N

Leon Dourge, 1934
Mietwohnhaus in Buenos Aires
Flats in Buenos Aires
Immeuble à Buenos Aires, vue d'en-
semble

Leon Dourge, 1933
Wohnanlage »Solaire« in Buenos
Aires, Ansicht von der Gartenseite
»Solaire« residential development
in Buenos Aires. View from the gar-
den
Complexe d'habitation »Solaire« à
Buenos Aires, vue du côté jardin

Bartolomé M. Repetto, 1936–1937
Mietwohnhaus in Buenos Aires,
Straßenseite
Flats in Buenos Aires. View from the
road
Immeuble à Buenos Aires, façade
donnant sur la rue

Bartolomé M. Repetto, 1936
Wohnhaus und Praxis eines Arztes
in Buenos Aires
Doctor's residence and practice in
Buenos Aires
Maison d'habitation et cabinet d'un
médecin à Buenos Aires

Bartolomé M. Repetto, 1936
Gruppe von drei Einfamilienhäu-
sern in Buenos Aires, Straßenseite
Group of three detached houses in
Buenos Aires. View from the road
Groupe de trois villas à Buenos
Aires, côté rue

Antonio U. Vilar, 1932
Gebäude des »Club Hindù« in
Buenos Aires, Sprungturm des
Schwimmbads
Swimming pool of »Club Hindù«
building in Buenos Aires. Diving-
board tower
Bâtiment du »Club Hindù« à Buenos
Aires, plongeoir de la piscine

Antonio U. Vilar, 1932
Gebäude des »Club Hindù« in
Buenos Aires, Schwimmbad im
Innenhof
»Club Hindù« building in Buenos
Aires, Swimmingpool
Bâtiment du »Club Hindù« à Buenos
Aires, piscine dans le patio

AUSTRALIEN

Stephenson, Meldrum und Turner, 1936
Gloucester-Gebäude des Royal Prince Alfred-Hospitals in Sydney
Gloucester building of the Royal Prince Alfred Hospital in Sydney
Bâtiment Gloucester de l'hôpital »Royal Prince Alfred« à Sydney

B E L G I E N

Victor Bourgeois, 1936
Villa »La Jeannerie« in Rhode
St. Genèse, Gartenseite
Villa »La Jeannerie« in Rhode
St. Genèse. View from the garden
Villa »La Jeannerie« à Rhode
St. Genèse, vue du côté jardin

Victor Bourgeois
Appartementhaus in Brüssel, Straßenfassade
Apartment building in Brussels. Street Facade
Immeuble d'appartements à Bruxelles, façade donnant sur la rue

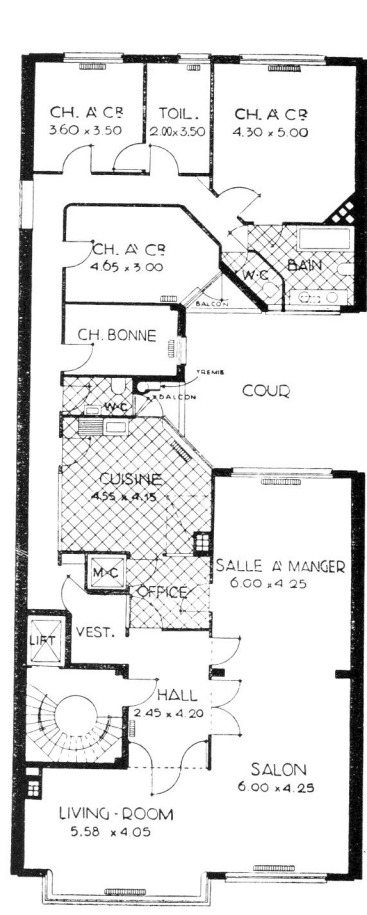

Victor Bourgeois
Appartementhaus in Brüssel, Grundriß einer Wohneinheit
Apartment building in Brussels. Ground plan of an apartment
Immeuble d'appartements à Bruxelles, plan d'une unité d'habitation

Gaston Eysselinck, 1933
Haus Peeters in Antwerpen, Süd-
seite
The Peeters House in Antwerp.
South view
Maison Peeters à Anvers, côté sud

Gaston Eysselinck, 1931
Haus des Architekten in Gent, Stra-
ßenseite
The architect's house in Ghent.
View from the road
Maison de l'architecte à Gand, côté
rue

Louis H. de Koninck, 1926
Haus des Malers Lenglet in Uccle,
Ostecke
The house of the painter Lenglet in
Uccle. East corner
Maison du peintre Lenglet à Uccle,
angle ouest

Louis H. de Koninck, 1926
Haus des Malers Lenglet in Uccle,
Nordecke
The house of the painter Lenglet in
Uccle. North corner
Maison du peintre Lenglet à Uccle,
angle nord

Louis H. de Koninck und A. Nyst, 1930
Reihenhaus in Lüttich, Straßenansicht; Grundrisse von Erdgeschoß und erstem Stock
Terrace house in Liège. View from the road; ground and first floor plans
Maison individuelle standard à Liège, vue côté rue; Plans du rez-de-chaussée et du premier étage

Louis H. de Koninck, 1931
Haus des Landschaftsarchitekten
Jean Marie Canneel in Auderghem,
Gartenseite
The house of the landscape
architect Jean Marie Canneel in
Auderghem. View from the garden
Maison de l'architecte paysagiste
Jean Marie Canneel à Auderghem,
côté jardin

Groupe L'Equerre, 1939
Pavillon der Universitäten auf der
Internationalen Ausstellung in
Lüttich, Südfassade
Universities Pavilion at the Inter-
national Exhibition in Liège. South
facade
Pavillon des Universités à l'Exposi-
tion Internationale de Liège; façade
sud

Groupe L'Equerre, 1939
Kindererholungsstätte auf der Internationalen Ausstellung in Lüttich, Gesamtansicht
Children's area at the International Exhibition in Liège. Overall view
Centre aéré pour enfants à l'Exposition Internationale de Liège; vue d'ensemble

Paul-Amaury Michel, 1935–1936
Wohnhaus in Brüssel, Straßenansicht
House in Brussels. View from the road
Immeuble à Bruxelles, façade donnant sur la rue

Paul-Amaury Michel, 1937
Mietwohnhaus in Brüssel, Straßenansicht
Flats in Brussels. View from the
road
Immeuble à Bruxelles, façade donnant sur la rue

BRASILIEN

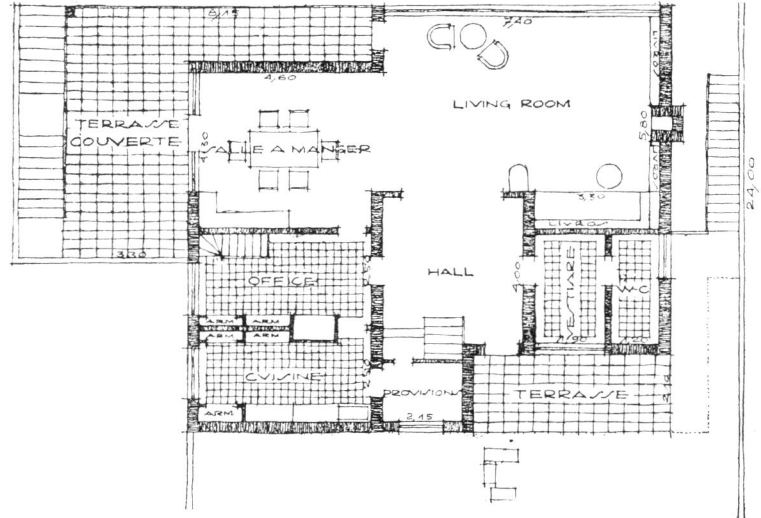

Gregori J. Warchavchik
Haus von Luiz da Silva Prado in São
Paulo, Südfassade; Grundriß des
Erdgeschosses
The house of Luiz da Silva Prado in
São Paulo. South facade; plan of
the ground floor
Maison de Luiz da Silva Prado à
São Paulo, façade sud; plan du rez-
de-chaussée

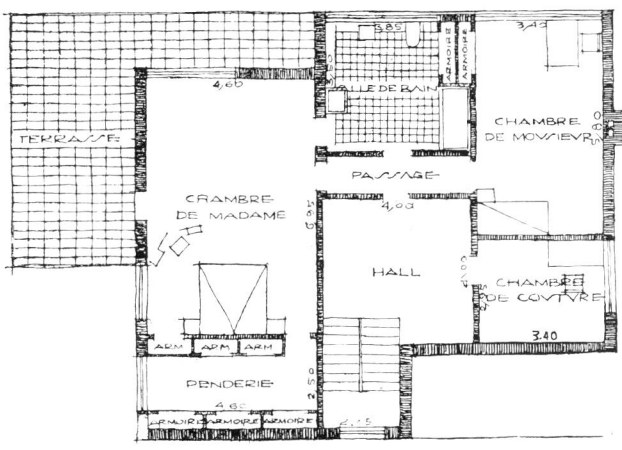

Gregori J. Warchavchik
Haus von Luiz da Silva Prado in São
Paulo, Nordseite; Grundriß des
ersten Stocks
The house of Luiz da Silva Prado in
São Paulo. North side; first-floor
plan
Maison de Luiz da Silva Prado à
São Paulo, côté nord; plan du pre-
mier étage

Gregori J. Warchavchik
Haus von Dr. Candido da Silva in
São Paulo, Ansichten
The house of Dr. Candido da Silva
in São Paulo, views
Maison du Dr Candido da Silva à
São Paulo, vues

Gregori J. Warchavchik
Einfamilienhaus in São Paulo, Straßenansicht
Detached house in São Paulo. View
from the road
Maison individuelle à São Paulo,
façade donnant sur la rue

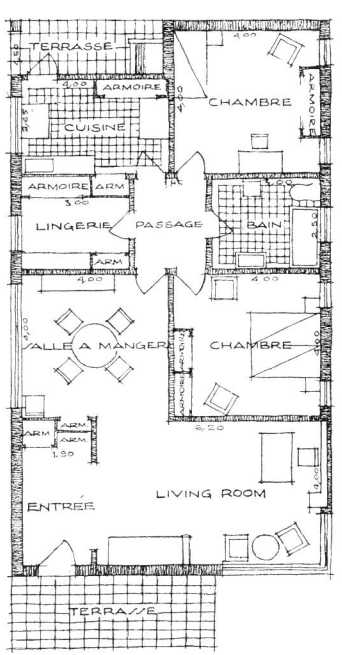

Gregori J. Warchavchik
Haus von Dr. Candido da Silva in
São Paulo, Grundriß
The house of Dr. Candido da Silva
in São Paulo. Ground plan
Maison du D^r. Candido da Silva à
São Paulo, plan

DÄNEMARK

Kay Fisker und Christian Frederik Møller, 1936–1938
Tuberkulosesanatorium für Kinder in Vordingborg, Hauptfassade
Tuberculosis sanatorium for children in Vordingborg. Main facade
Sanatorium pour enfants tuberculeux à Vordingborg, façade principale

Poul Holsöe, 1938
Grundschule in der Siedlung
Bispebjerg in Grundtvig, Gesamt-
ansicht und Hauptfassade
Elementary school at Bispebjerg in
Grundtvig. Overall view and main
facade
Ecole primaire dans le lotissement
Bispebjerg à Grundtvig, vue d'en-
semble et façade principale

**Kay Fisker und Christian Frederik
Møller, 1937–1938**
Wohnsiedlung in Kopenhagen
Housing estate in Copenhagen
Lotissement à Copenhague

Arne Jacobsen
Sporthalle in Hellerup, Kopen-
hagen, Tennisplatz
Sports complex at Hellerup,
Copenhagen. Tennis court
Halle des sports à Hellerup,
Copenhague, court de tennis

Arne Jacobsen, 1932
Wohnsiedlung Bellavista in
Klampenborg, Kopenhagen, Blick
vom Hof zum Meer
Bellavista housing estate in Klampenborg, Copenhagen. View from
the courtyard towards the sea
Lotissement Bellavista à Klampenborg, Copenhague, vue de la cour
sur la mer

Arne Jacobsen, 1932
Wohnsiedlung Bellavista in
Klampenborg, Kopenhagen, Straßenansicht
Bellavista housing estate in Klampenborg, Copenhagen. View from
the road
Lotissement Bellavista à Klampenborg, Copenhague, vue de la rue

Arne Jacobsen, 1932
Wohnsiedlung Bellavista in Klam-
penborg, Kopenhagen, Eck einer
Wohnzeile
Bellavista housing estate in
Klampenborg, Copenhagen.
Corner of a housing block
Lotissement Bellavista à Klampen-
borg, Copenhague, extrémité d'une
rangée d'habitation

DEUTSCHLAND

Marcel Breuer, 1932
Haus Harnischmacher in Wies-
baden, Südseite
The Harnischmacher House in
Wiesbaden. South side
Maison Harnischmacher à Wiesba-
den, côté sud

Richard Döcker, 1927–1928
Haus Dr. K. in Stuttgart, Ansicht mit
Gartenterrasse
The house of Dr. K. in Stuttgart.
View showing garden terrace
Maison du D' K. à Stuttgart, vue de
face avec terrasse de jardin

Richard Döcker, 1927–1928
Haus Dr. K. in Stuttgart, Blick zum
überdachten Freiplatz
The house of Dr. K. in Stuttgart.
View of covered open-air area
Maison du D' K. à Stuttgart, vue sur
terrain couvert

Richard Döcker, 1926–1928
Bezirkskrankenhaus Waiblingen, Zweibettzimmer mit Blick auf die Terrasse
District hospital in Waiblingen. Double room with a view of the terrace
Hôpital régional de Waiblingen, chambre à deux lits avec vue sur la terrasse

Richard Döcker, 1926–1928
Bezirkskrankenhaus Waiblingen,
Terrasse mit Sonnenplätzen für die
Patienten. Die Fenster über dem
vorspringenden Schutzdach
beleuchten das Krankenzimmer.
District hospital in Waiblingen. Sun
terrace for patients. The windows
above the projecting roof give light
to the ward.
Hôpital régional de Waibligen, terrasse avec places au soleil pour les
patients. Les fenêtres au-dessus du
toit de protection en saillie éclairent
la chambre des malades.

Richard Döcker, 1926–1928
Bezirkskrankenhaus Waiblingen,
»Tagraumbalkone«, vom Opera-
tionsbau aus gesehen.
District hospital in Waiblingen. The
dayroom balconies seen from the
operating-theatre building.
Hôpital régional de Waiblingen,
»balcons-salles de séjour« vus du
bâtiment d'opération.

Fred Forbat, 1931
Wohnsiedlung »Siemensstadt« in
Berlin, Bauteil VI a, Westfassade
»Siemensstadt« housing estate in
Berlin. West facade of block VI a
Lotissement »Siemensstadt« à Ber-
lin, bâtiment VI a, façade ouest

Fred Forbat, 1931
Wohnsiedlung »Siemensstadt« in
Berlin, Bauteil VI a und b
»Siemensstadt« housing estate in
Berlin. Blocks VI a and VI b
Lotissement »Siemensstadt« à Ber-
lin, bâtiment VI a et b

Walter Gropius, 1931
Wohnsiedlung »Siemensstadt« in
Berlin, Bauteil mit 2½-Zimmer-
Wohnungen, Westfassade
»Siemensstadt« housing estate in
Berlin. Block of 2½ room apart-
ments; west view
Lotissement »Siemensstadt« à Ber-
lin, bâtiment avec appartements
2½ pièces, façade ouest

Walter Gropius, 1925–1926
Das Bauhaus in Dessau, Gesamtansicht; Durchfahrt und Glasfas-
sade des Werkstattbaus
The Bauhaus in Dessau. Overall
view. Access way and glass facade
of the workshop building
Le Bauhaus à Dessau, vue d'ensemble; passage et façade de verre du
bâtiment des ateliers

Walter Gropius, 1925–1926
Doppelhaus für Bauhausmeister in
Dessau, Südseite
Semi-detached house for Bauhaus
masters in Dessau. South side
Maison à deux habitations pour
maîtres du Bauhaus à Dessau, côté
sud

Walter Gropius, 1925–1926
Das Bauhaus in Dessau, Studenten-
wohnheim
The Bauhaus in Dessau. Student's
dormitory block
Le Bauhaus à Dessau, foyer d'étudiants

Walter Gropius, 1928
Gebäude des Konsumvereins in der
Siedlung Dessau-Törten, Gesamt-
ansicht
Building of the Consumers'
Cooperative in the housing estate at
Törten, Dessau. Overall View
Bâtiment de l'Association des
Consommateurs dans le lotissement
Dessau-Törten, vue d'ensemble

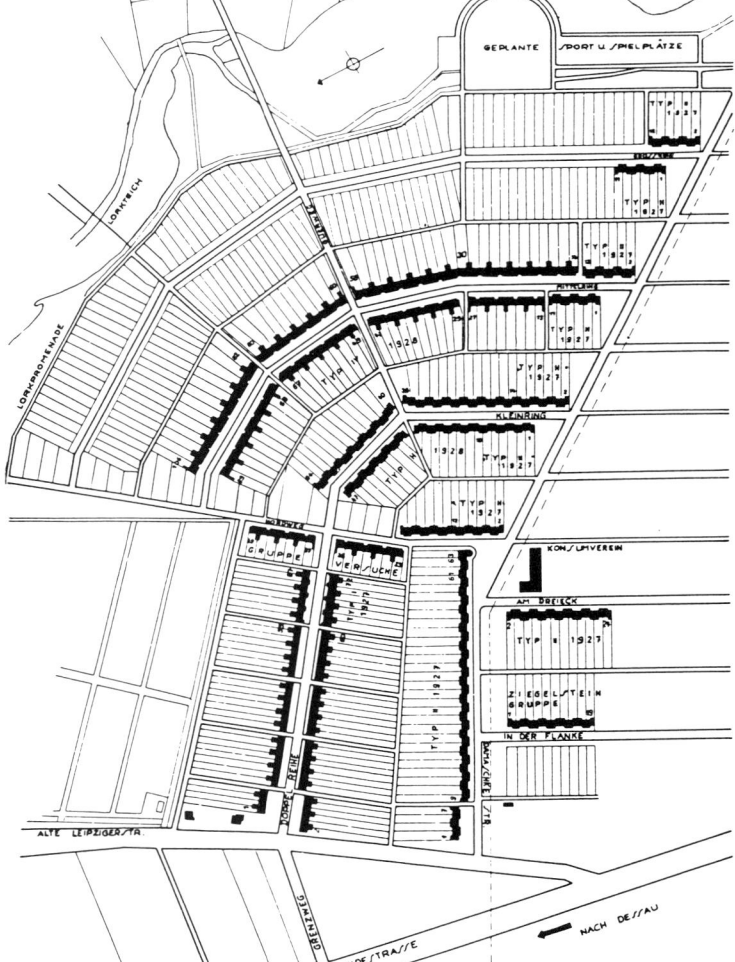

Walter Gropius, 1925–1928
Siedlung Dessau-Törten, Gesamt-
plan
Housing estate at Törten, Dessau.
Overall plan
Lotissement Dessau-Törten, plan de
l'ensemble

Walter Gropius, 1928
Siedlung Dessau-Törten, Reihen-
häuser
Housing estate at Törten, Dessau.
Terrace houses
Lotissement Dessau-Törten, habita-
tions individuelles standard

Walter Gropius, 1929
Siedlung Dammerstock in Karls-
ruhe, Gruppe 5, Westfassade
Dammerstock housing estate in
Karlsruhe. Group 5, West facade
Lotissement Dammerstock à Karls-
ruhe, groupe 5, façade ouest

Walter Gropius, 1929
Laubenganghaus in der Siedlung
Dammerstock in Karlsruhe,
Gruppe 6, Ostfassade
Apartment block in the Dammer-
stock housing estate in Karlsruhe.
Group 6, East facade
Immeuble à galeries couvertes
dans le lotissement Dammerstock à
Karlsruhe, groupe 6, façade est

Otto Haesler, 1929
Kleinwohnungsanlage mit Wasch-
haus in der Siedlung Dammerstock
in Karlsruhe
Small residential units with wash-
house in the Dammerstock housing
estate in Karlsruhe
Ensemble de petits appartements
avec pavillon buanderie dans le
lotissement Dammerstock à Karlsruhe

Otto Haesler und Karl Völker, 1932
Altenwohnheim in Kassel, Südflügel
Old people's home in Kassel. South
wing
Maison de retraite à Kassel, aile
sud

Otto Haesler und Karl Völker, 1932
Altenwohnheim in Kassel, Gesamt-
ansicht mit Haupteingang
Old people's home in Kassel.
Overall view showing main entr-
ance
Maison de retraite à Kassel, vue
d'ensemble avec entrée principale

Otto Haesler und Karl Völker, 1932
Altenwohnheim in Kassel, Ansicht
des Südflügels
Old people's home in Kassel. View
of south wing
Maison de retraite à Kassel, vue de
l'aile sud

Otto Haesler, 1929
Volksschule in Celle, Aula
Assembly hall of the elementary
school in Celle
Ecole communale à Celle, salle des
fêtes

Otto Haesler
Siedlung Georgsgarten in Celle,
Teil der Hauptfassade
Georgsgarten housing estate in
Celle. Part of the main facade
Lotissement Georgsgarten à Celle,
partie de la façade principale

Le Corbusier und Pierre Jeanneret, 1927
Zwei Häuser in der Weißenhofsiedlung in Stuttgart
Two houses in the Weissenhof
housing estate in Stuttgart
Deux maisons du lotissement Weißenhof à Stuttgart

Le Corbusier und Pierre Jeanneret, 1927
Haus in der Weißenhofsiedlung in
Stuttgart, Dachgarten
House in the Weissenhof housing
estate in Stuttgart. Roof garden
Maison du lotissement Weißenhof à
Stuttgart, toit en terrasse

**Le Corbusier und Pierre Jeanneret,
1927**
Haus in der Weißenhofsiedlung in
Stuttgart, Straßenseite
House in the Weissenhof housing
estate in Stuttgart. View from the
road
Maison du lotissement Weißenhof à
Stuttgart, vue de la façade donnant
sur la rue

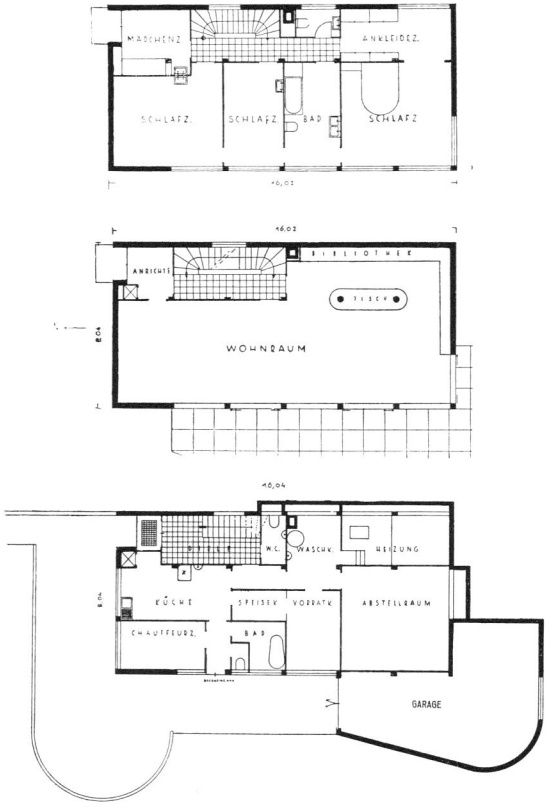

**Hans und Wassili Luckhardt mit
Alfons Anker, 1929**
Villa am Rupenhorn, Berlin, Ansicht
und Grundrisse
Villa am Rupenhorn, Berlin. View
and floor plans
Villa à Rupenhorn, Berlin, vue de
face et plans

Hans und Wassili Luckhardt, 1932
Villa F. in Velten bei Berlin, Gartenseite
Villa F. in Velten near Berlin. View
from the garden
Villa F. à Velten près de Berlin, côté
jardin

Ernst May und E. Kaufmann, 1927–1929
Gaststätte und Vereinshaus in der Siedlung Praunheim in Frankfurt/Main
Restaurant and clubhouse in the Praunheim housing estate in Frankfurt/Main
Restaurant et club du lotissement Praunheim à Francfort/Main

Ernst May, H. Boehm und C. H. Rudloff, 1926–1927
Siedlung Höhenblick in Frankfurt/Main
Höhenblick housing estate in Frankfurt/Main
Lotissement Höhenblick à Francfort/Main

**Ernst May und C. H. Rudloff,
1927–1928**
Siedlung Römerstadt in Frank-
furt/Main
Römerstadt housing estate in
Frankfurt/Main
Lotissement Römerstadt à Franc-
fort/Main

**Ernst May, H. Boehm und
C. H. Rudloff, 1926–1927**
Siedlung Bruchfeldstraße in Frank-
furt/Main
Bruchfeldstraße housing estate in
Frankfurt/Main
Lotissement Bruchfeldstraße à
Francfort/Main

Erich Mendelsohn, 1926
Kaufhaus Schocken in Nürnberg,
Verkaufsraum im Obergeschoß
Schocken department store in
Nuremberg. Sales area on upper
floor
Grand magasin Schocken à
Nuremberg, salle de ventes du pre-
mier étage

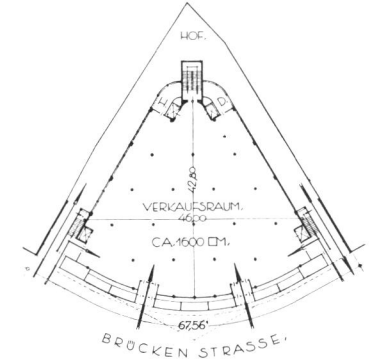

Erich Mendelsohn, 1928–1929
Kaufhaus Schocken in Chemnitz,
Straßenfront und Grundriß
Schocken department store in
Chemnitz. Facade and ground plan
Grand magasin Schocken à Chem-
nitz, façade donnant sur la rue et
plan

Ludwig Mies van der Rohe, 1927
Mietwohnhaus in der Weißenhofsiedlung in Stuttgart, Straßenseite
Flats in the Weissenhof housing
estate in Stuttgart. View from the
road
Immeuble du lotissement Weißenhof à Stuttgart, côté rue

Jacobus Johannes Pieter Oud, 1927
Reihenhäuser in der Weißenhofsiedlung in Stuttgart; im Hintergrund das Haus von Walter Gropius, links der Block von Mies van
der Rohe
Terrace houses in the Weissenhof
housing estate in Stuttgart. In the
background, the Walter Gropius
house. To the left, the Mies van der
Rohe block
Maisons d'habitation individuelles
standard du lotissement Weißenhof
à Stuttgart; dans le fond, la maison
de Walter Gropius, à gauche, le
bloc de Mies van der Rohe

Mart Stam, 1927
Reihenhäuser in der Weißenhofsiedlung in Stuttgart; im Hintergrund der Block von Mies van der
Rohe
Terrace houses in the Weissenhof
housing estate in Stuttgart. In the
background, the Mies van der Rohe
block
Maisons d'habitation individuelles
standard du lotissement Weißenhof
à Stuttgart; dans le fond, le bloc de
Mies van der Rohe

Adolf Rading, 1930
Wohnhaus und Praxis von Dr. Rabe
in Zwenkau, Ansichten; Grundrisse
von Erdgeschoß und Obergeschoß
Residence and practice of Dr. Rabe
in Zwenkau. Views; ground-floor
and first-floor plan
Immeuble et cabinet du Dr Rabe à
Zwenkau, vues; plans du rez-de-
chaussée et du premier étage

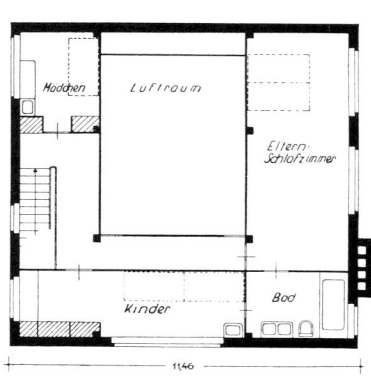

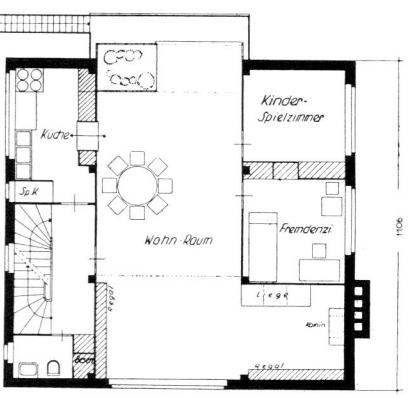

Adolf Rading, 1930
Wohnhaus und Praxis von Dr. Rabe
in Zwenkau, Halle mit Wandgestal-
tung von Oskar Schlemmer
Residence and practice of Dr. Rabe
in Zwenkau. Hall with wall design
by Oskar Schlemmer
Immeuble et cabinet du Dr Rabe à
Zwenkau, hall avec décoration
murale d'Oskar Schlemmer

Hans Scharoun, 1930
Wohnsiedlung »Siemensstadt« in
Berlin, Ansicht der Gartenseite
»Siemensstadt« housing estate in
Berlin. View from the garden
Lotissement »Siemensstadt« à Ber-
lin, vue du côté jardin

Hans Scharoun, 1930
Wohnsiedlung »Siemensstadt« in
Berlin, Ansicht der Straßenseite
»Siemensstadt« housing estate in
Berlin. View from the road
Lotissement »Siemensstadt« à Ber-
lin, vue du côté rue

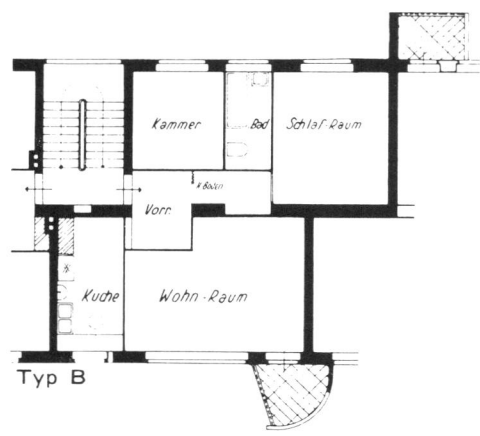

Hans Scharoun, 1930
Wohnsiedlung »Siemensstadt« in
Berlin, Ansicht der Straßenseite mit
Ladengeschäften; Grundriß einer
Wohneinheit
»Siemensstadt« housing estate in
Berlin. View from the road showing
shops; ground plan for a residential
unit
Lotissement »Siemensstadt« à Ber-
lin, vue du côté rue avec vitrines de
magasins; plan d'un logement

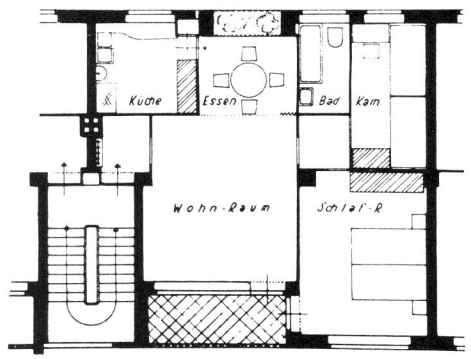

Hans Scharoun, 1930
Wohnsiedlung »Siemensstadt« in
Berlin, Ansicht der Gartenseite;
Grundriß einer Wohneinheit
»Siemensstadt« housing estate in
Berlin. View from the garden;
ground plan for a residential unit
Lotissement »Siemensstadt« à Ber-
lin, vue du côté jardin; plan d'un
logement

Hans Scharoun, 1933
Villa Schmincke in Löbau, Sachsen,
Gartenseite
The Schmincke Villa in Löbau, Sax-
ony. View from the garden
Villa Schmincke à Löbau, Saxe,
côté jardin

Hans Scharoun, 1933
Villa Schmincke in Löbau, Sachsen,
Nordseite
The Schmincke Villa in Löbau, Saxony. North side
Villa Schmincke à Löbau, Saxe,
côté nord

Hans Scharoun, 1933
Villa Schmincke in Löbau, Sachsen,
Wintergarten
The Schmincke Villa in Löbau, Saxony. Winter garden
Villa Schmincke à Löbau, Saxe, jardin d'hiver

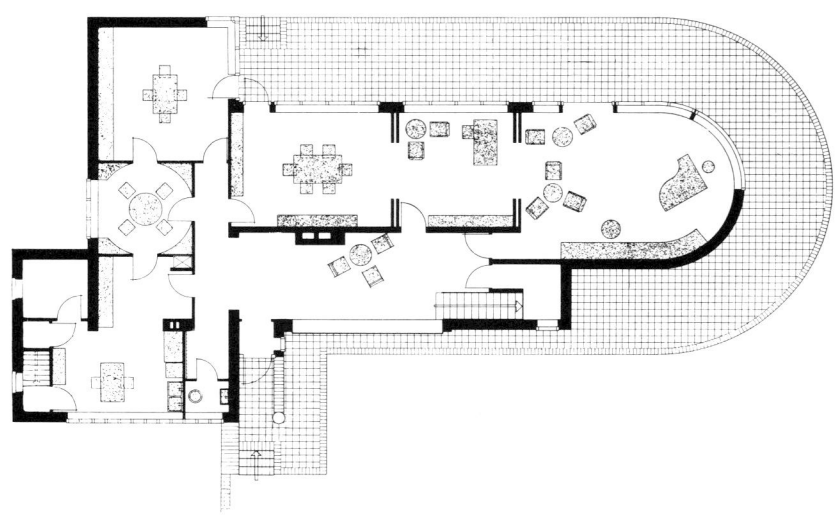

Karl Schneider, 1927–1928
Villa Römer in Hamburg/Altona,
Südseite; Erdgeschoßgrundriß
The Römer Villa in Altona, Hamburg. South side; ground-floor plan
The Römer Villa à Hambourg/
Altona, côté sud; plan du rez-de-chaussée

Karl Schneider, 1927–1928
Villa Römer in Hamburg/Altona,
Nordseite; Obergeschoßgrundriß
The Römer Villa in Altona, Hamburg. North side; plan of upper
floor
Villa Römer à Hambourg/Altona,
côté nord; plan du premier étage

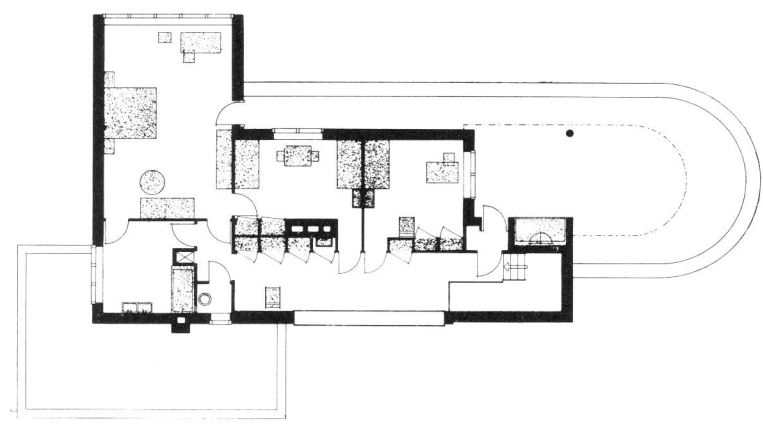

Karl Schneider, 1930
Kunstausstellungsgebäude in Hamburg, Haupteingang
Art exhibition building in Hamburg.
Main entrance
Bâtiment d'exposition d'art à Hambourg, entrée principale

Karl Schneider, 1930
Kunstausstellungsgebäude in Hamburg, Eingang, von innen gesehen
Art exhibition building in Hamburg.
Interior view of entrance
Bâtiment d'exposition d'art à Hambourg, entrée vue de l'intérieur

Karl Schneider, 1930
Kunstausstellungsgebäude in Hamburg, Blick in den großen Ausstellungssaal; Variationen des Stellwandsystems
Art exhibition building in Hamburg. View into the main exhibition room; variations of the partitioning system
Bâtiment d'exposition d'art à Hambourg, vue dans la grande salle d'exposition; variations du système de parois

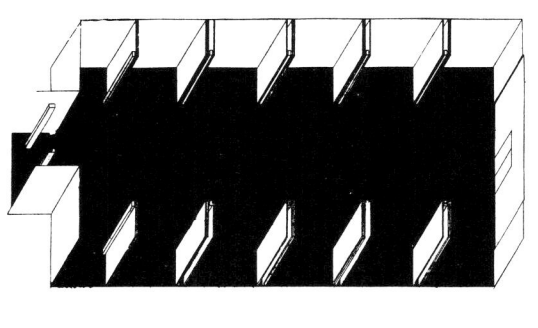
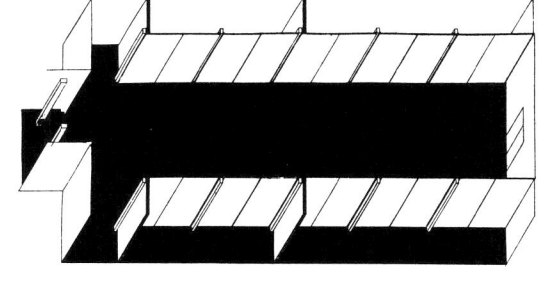

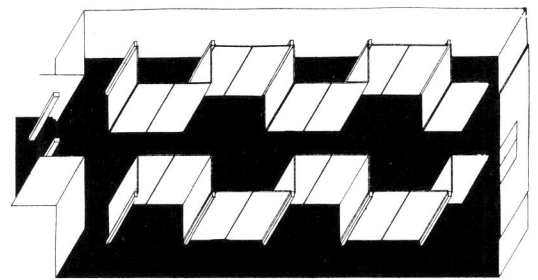

Otto Ernst Schweizer, 1926–1928
Sportstadion in Nürnberg, Rück-
front des Tribünenhauses
Sports stadium in Nuremberg. Rear
view of grandstand
Stade de Nuremberg, façade postérieure du bâtiment des tribunes

Otto Ernst Schweizer, 1926–1928
Sportstadion in Nürnberg, Vorhalle
im Tribünenbau
Sports stadium in Nuremberg. Front
hall of grandstand
Stade de Nuremberg, hall d'entrée
du bâtiment des tribunes

Otto Ernst Schweizer, 1926–1928
Sportstadion in Nürnberg, Tribüne
Sports stadium in Nuremberg.
Grandstand
Stade de Nuremberg, tribunes

Hans Wittwer, 1931
Flugplatzrestaurant in Schkeuditz,
Zufahrt
Airport restaurant in Schkeuditz.
Entrance
Restaurant de l'aérodrome de
Schkeuditz, entrée

Hans Wittwer, 1931
Flugplatzrestaurant in Schkeuditz,
vom Rollfeld aus gesehen
Airport restaurant in Schkeuditz.
View from the runway
Restaurant de l'aérodrome de
Schkeuditz, vu de la piste

FINNLAND

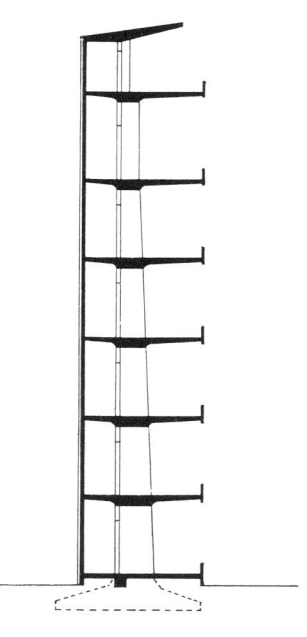

Alvar Aalto, 1932
Tuberkulosesanatorium in Paimio,
Gesamtansicht von Osten; Quer-
schnitt durch den Trakt mit den Son-
nenterrassen
Tuberculosis sanatorium in Paimio.
Overall view from the east; cross
section of the sun-terrace wing
Sanatorium de Paimio, vue d'ensemble du côté est; coupe de l'aile
comprenant les terrasses solarium

Alvar Aalto, 1932
Tuberkulosesanatorium in Paimio,
Flügel mit Krankenzimmern
Tuberculosis sanatorium in Paimio.
Ward wing
Sanatorium de Paimio, aile com-
prenant les chambres des malades

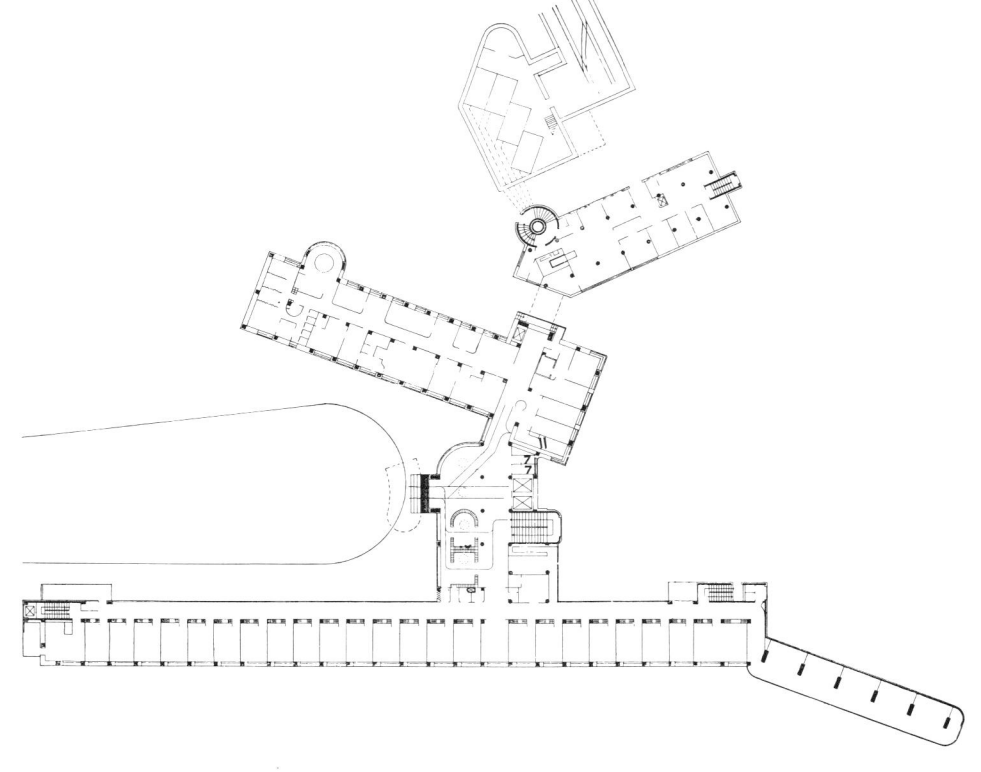

Alvar Aalto, 1932
Tuberkulosesanatorium in Paimio,
Sonnenterrasse; Gesamtplan
Tuberculosis sanatorium in Paimio.
Sun terrace; overall plan
Sanatorium de Paimio, terrasse
solarium; plan complet

Alvar Aalto, 1934
Haus des Architekten in Helsinki,
Gartenansicht
The architect's house in Helsinki.
View from the garden
Maison de l'architecte à Helsinki,
vue côté jardin

Alvar Aalto, 1934
Haus des Architekten in Helsinki,
Eingang
The architect's house in Helsinki.
Entrance
Maison de l'architecte à Helsinki,
entrée

Alvar Aalto, 1928–1929
Gebäude der Zeitung »Turun Sanomat« in Aabo, Straßenansicht
»Turun Sanomat« newspaper building in Aabo. View from the road
Bâtiment du journal »Turun Sanomat« à Aabo, vue côté rue

A. Hythönen und R. V. Luukkonen
Gebäude der Mustermesse in Helsinki, Gesamtansicht
Trade Fair building in Helsinki.
Overall view
Bâtiment de la foire modèle à Helsinki, vue d'ensemble

A. Hythönen und R. V. Luukkonen
Gebäude der Mustermesse in Helsinki, Eingangsfront
Trade Fair building in Helsinki.
Entrance frontage
Bâtiment de la foire modèle à Helsinki, façade de l'entrée

FRANKREICH

Pierre Chareau, 1931–1932
Wohnhaus und Praxis von Dr. Jean
Dalsace in Paris, Gartenseite
Residence and practice of Dr. Jean
Dalsace in Paris. View from the
garden
Maison d'habitation et cabinet du
Dr Jean Dalsace à Paris, côté jardin

Pierre Chareau, 1931–1932
Wohnhaus und Praxis von Dr. Jean
Dalsace in Paris, Aufgang zum
Galeriegeschoß
Residence and practice of Dr. Jean
Dalsace in Paris. Way up to gallery
floor
Maison d'habitation et cabinet du
Dʳ Jean Dalsace à Paris, montée
vers l'étage de la galerie

Gabriel Guevrekian, 1926
Villa J. Heim in Neuilly, Paris, Terrasse im ersten Stock; Gartenseite
The villa J. Heim in Neuilly, Paris. First-floor patio; view from the garden
Villa J. Heim à Neuil y, Paris, terrasse au premier étage; côté jardin

Gabriel Guevrekian, 1926
Villa J. Heim in Neuilly, Paris,
Dachgarten
The villa J. Heim in Neuilly, Paris.
Roof garden
Villa J. Heim à Neuilly, Paris, toit en
terrasse

Le Corbusier und Pierre Jeanneret, 1923
Villa La Roche und Jeanneret in Auteuil, Paris, Eingangsseite
The Villa of La Roche and Jeanneret in Auteuil, Paris. Entrance side
Villa La Roche et Jeanneret à Auteuil, Paris, côté de l'entrée

Le Corbusier und Pierre Jeanneret, 1928–1929
Villa Church in Ville d'Avray, Dachgarten
The Church Villa in Vi le d'Avray. Roof garden
Villa Church à Ville d'Avray, toit en terrasse

**Le Corbusier und Pierre Jeanneret,
1927**
Villa Stein in Garches, Nordfassade; Dachgarten
The Stein Villa in Garches. North facade. Roof garden
Villa Stein à Garches, façade nord; toit en terrase

Le Corbusier und Pierre Jeanneret, 1927
Villa Stein in Garches, Nordfassade mit Garagentor und Vordach
The Stein Villa in Garches. North facade with garage door and canopy roof
Villa Stein à Garches, façade nord avec portail et avancée de toit

**Le Corbusier und Pierre Jeanneret,
1927**
Villa Stein in Garches, Innenansicht
The Stein Villa in Garches. Interior
view
Villa Stein à Garches, vue intérieure

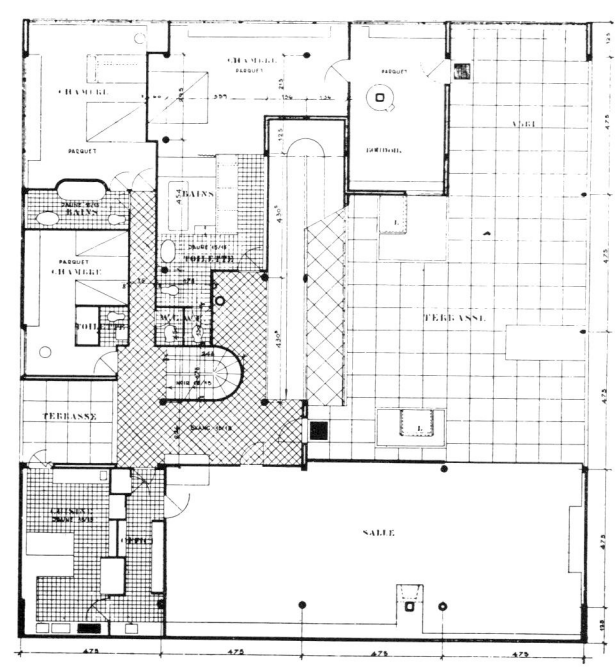

Le Corbusier und Pierre Jeanneret, 1931
Villa Savoye in Poissy, Ostfassade;
Grundriß des ersten Stocks
The Savoye Villa in Poissy. East
facade; ground plan of first floor
Villa Savoye à Poissy, façade est;
plan du premier étage

Le Corbusier und Pierre Jeanneret, 1931
Villa Savoye in Poissy, Eingang mit Pilotis; Grundriß des Erdgeschosses
The Savoye Villa in Poissy. Entrance with pilotis. Plan of ground floor
Villa Savoye à Poissy, entrée avec pilotis; plan du rez-de-chaussée

**Le Corbusier und Pierre Jeanneret,
1931**
Villa Savoye in Poissy, Innenansicht
des ersten Stocks mit Treppe und
Ausgang zur Rampe
The Savoye Villa in Poissy. Interior
view of first floor showing staircase
and exit to ramp
Villa Savoye à Poissy, vue intérieure
du premier étage avec escalier et
sortie vers la rampe

**Le Corbusier und Pierre Jeanneret,
1931**
Villa Savoye in Poissy, Eingang, von
innen gesehen
The Savoye Villa in Poissy. Interior
view of entrance
Villa Savoye à Poissy, entrée vue de
l'intérieur

Le Corbusier und Pierre Jeanneret, 1931
Villa Savoye in Poissy, Rampe zwischen den Dachterrassen
The Savoye Villa in Poissy. Ramp between the roof terraces
Villa Savoye à Poissy, rampe entre les terrasses du toit

Le Corbusier und Pierre Jeanneret, 1932
Schweizer Pavillon der Universität in Paris
Swiss pavilion of the university of Paris
Pavillon suisse de l'Université de Paris

Le Corbusier und Pierre Jeanneret, 1932
Schweizer Pavillon der Universität in Paris, Nordseite mit Treppenturm
Swiss pavilion of the university of Paris. North side with stairwell tower
Pavillon suisse de l'Université de Paris, côté nord avec tour d'escaliers

Le Corbusier und Pierre Jeanneret, 1932
Schweizer Pavillon der Universität in Paris, Südfassade
Swiss pavilion of the university of Paris. South facade
Pavillon suisse de l'Université de Paris, façade sud

Le Corbusier und Pierre Jeanneret, 1933
Gebäude der Heilsarmee in Paris, Haupteingang
Salvation Army building in Paris. Main entrance
Bâtiment de l'Armée du Salut à Paris, entrée principale

André Lurçat, 1931–1932
Villa Hefferlin in Ville d'Avray, Süd-
seite
The Hefferlin Villa in Ville d'Avray.
South side
Villa Hefferlin à Ville d'Avray, côté
sud

André Lurçat, 1931–1932
Haus Guggenbuhl am Parc de
Montsouris in Paris
The Guggenbuhl house on the Parc
de Montsouris in Paris
Maison Guggenbuhl au bord du
parc de Montsouris à Paris

André Lurçat, 1932
Schule in Villejuif
School in Villejuif
Ecole à Villejuif

André Lurçat, 1932
Schule in Villejuif, Pausenhof der
Knabenschule
School in Villejuif. Boys' play-
ground
Ecole à Villejuif, cour de récréation
de l'école de garçons

André Lurçat, 1932
Schule in Villejuif, Turnhalle
School in Villejuif. Gymnasium
Ecole à Villejuif, gymnase

André Lurçat, 1931
Künstlerhotel »Nord-Süd« in Calvi
auf Korsika, Ostseite
Artists' hotel »North-South« in
Calvi, Corsica. View from the east
Hôtel des artistes »Nord-Sud« à
Calvi en Corse, côté est

Georges-Henri Pingusson, 1931
Pension »Latitude 43« in Saint-
Tropez, Ansicht von Westen
»Latitude 43« pension in St. Tropez.
View from the west
Pension »Latitude 43« à Saint-Tro-
pez, vue de l'ouest

GRIECHENLAND

Pericle Georgacopoulos
Mietwohnhaus in Athen
Flats in Athens
Immeuble à Athènes

J. G. Despotopulos
Tuberkulosesanatorium bei Athen,
Südostfassade
Tuberculosis sanatorium near
Athens. South-east facade
Sanatorium près d'Athènes, façade
sud-est

J. G. Despotopulos
Tuberkulosesanatorium bei Athen,
Sonnenterrasse
Tuberculosis sanatorium near
Athens. Sun terrace
Sanatorium près d'Athènes, ter-
rasse solarium

Patrocle Karantinos
Grundschule in Tambouria, Piräus,
Hauptfassade
Elementary school in Tambouria,
Piraeus. Main facade
Ecole primaire à Tambouria, Pirée,
façade principale

Patrocle Karantinos
Grundschule unterhalb der Akro-
polis in Athen, Südfassade
Elementary school below the
Acropolis in Athens. South facade
Ecole primaire au-dessous de
l'Acropole à Athènes, façade sud

Patrocle Karantinos
Grundschule in Harakopou, Athen,
Südfassade
Elementary school in Harakopou,
Athens. South facade
Ecole primaire à Harakopou,
Athènes, façade sud

Patrocle Karantinos
Grundschule in Tambouria, Piräus,
Haupteingang
Elementary school in Tambouria,
Piraeus. Main entrance
Ecole primaire à Tambouria, Pirée,
entrée principale

Stamo Papadaki, 1933
Villa am Meer in Glyfada, Nord-
und Südseite
Seaside villa in Glyfada. North and
south sides
Villa au bord de la mer à Glyfada,
côtés nord et sud

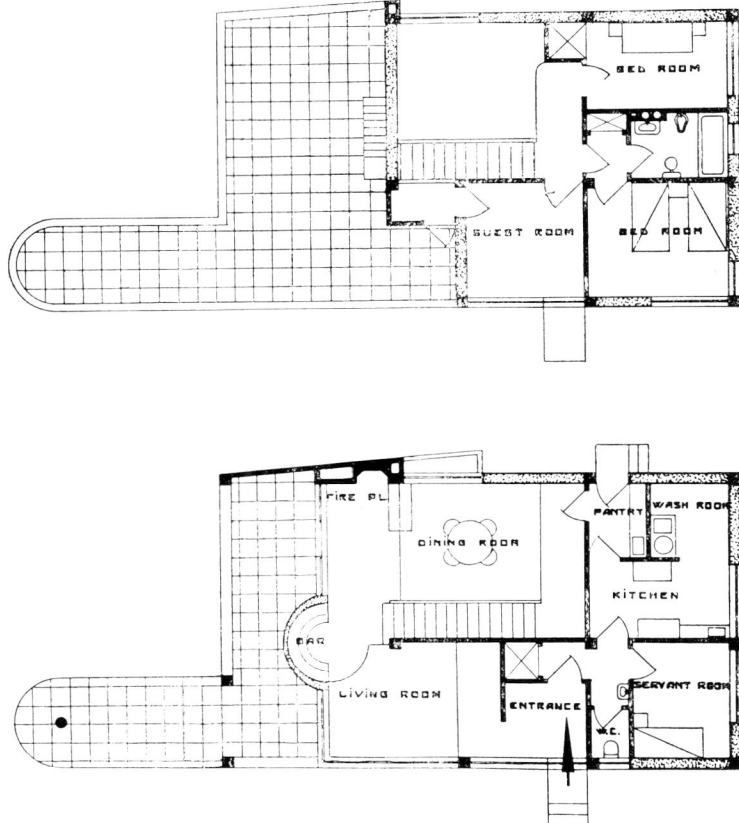

Stamo Papadaki, 1933
Villa am Meer in Glyfada, Seeseite;
Grundrisse von Erdgeschoß und
erstem Stock
Seaside villa in Glyfada. View from
the sea; ground-floor and first-floor
plans
Villa au bord de la mer à Glyfada,
côté de la mer; plans du rez-de-
chaussée et du premier étage

GROSSBRITANNIEN

**A. Chitty, L. Drake, M. Dugdale,
V. Harding, B. Lubetkin, G. Samuel
und F. Skinner (Tecton), 1933**
Gorillahaus des Regent's Park Zoo
in London
Gorilla house at Regent's Park Zoo
in London
Maison des gorilles au zoo du
Regent's Park à Londres

Wells Coates, 1932–1934
Kleinwohnungsanlage in Hamp-
stead, London, Nordseite mit Lau-
bengängen
Apartment block in Hampstead,
London. North side with access Bal-
conies
Ensemble de petits appartements à
Hampstead, Londres, côté nord
avec galeries couvertes

Wells Coates, 1934–1935
Apartmenthaus »Embassy Court« in
Brighton, Sussex, Straßenseite
»Embassy Court« apartment build-
ing in Brighton, Sussex. View from
the road
Immeuble de studios »Embassy
Court« à Brighton, Sussex, côté rue

Wells Coates, 1934–1935
Apartmenthaus »Embassy Court« in
Brighton, Sussex, Rückseite
»Embassy Court« apartment build-
ing in Brighton, Sussex. Courtyard
side
Immeuble de studios »Embassy
Court« à Brighton, Sussex, côté
cour

Patrick Gwynne und Wells Coates, 1933
Villa »The Homewood« von A. L. Gwynne in Esher, Surrey, Ansicht des Flügels mit Wohn- und Eßzimmer
»The Homewood«. Residence of A. L. Gwynne in Esher, Surrey. View of the dining-room and living-room wing
Villa »The Homewood« de A. L. Gwynne à Esher, Surrey, vue sur l'aile comprenant les salles de séjour et à manger

Patrick Gwynne und Wells Coates, 1933
Villa »The Homewood« von A. L. Gwynne in Esher, Surrey, Ansicht des Flügels mit den Schlafzimmern
»The Homewood« villa of A. L. Gwynne in Esher, Surrey. View of the bedroom wing
Villa »The Homewood« de A. L. Gwynne à Esher, Surrey, vue de l'aile comprenant les chambres à coucher

Wells Coates, 1934–1936
Landhaus in Benfleet, Essex, Gartenseite
Country house at Benfleet, Essex. View from the garden
Maison de campagne à Benfleet, Essex, côté jardin

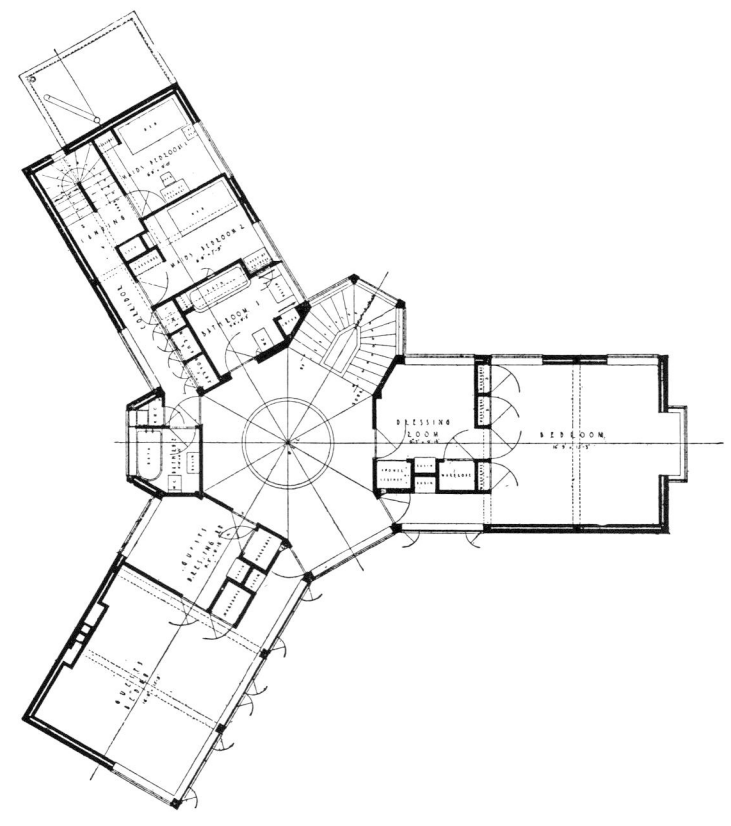

**Amyas Douglas Connell, Basil
Robert Ward und Colin Anderson
Lucas, 1930**
Landhaus in Amersham, Bucking-
hamshire, Südwestansicht; Grund-
riß des ersten Stocks
Country house in Amersham, Buck-
inghamshire. South-west view; first-
floor plan
Maison de campagne à Amersham,
Buckinghamshire, vue du sud-est;
plan du premier étage

Amyas Douglas Connell, Basil Robert Ward und Colin Anderson Lucas, 1930
Landhaus in Amersham, Buckinghamshire, Transformatorenhaus, im Hintergrund links die Pförtnerwohnung, rechts das Hauptgebäude (oben); Wasserturm mit Aussichtsterrasse und Ballspielplatz (unten)
Country house in Amersham, Buckinghamshire. Transformer house. In the background, the caretaker's accommodation and the main building (above). Water tower with therrace and ball games court (below)
Maison de campagne à Amersham, Buckinghamshire, maison des transformateurs, au fond à gauche l'appartement du gardien, à droite le bâtiment principal; château d'eau avec terrasse et terrain de jeu (en bas)

**Amyas Douglas Connell und Basil
Robert Ward, 1932**
Landhaus »New Farm« in Grays-
wood, Haslemere, Surrey, West-
seite mit gläsernem Treppenhaus
»New Farm« country house at
Grayswood, Haslemere, Surrey.
West side with glass stairwell,
Maison de campagne »New Farm«
à Grayswood, Haslemere, Surrey,
côté ouest avec montée d'escalier
en verre

**Amyas Douglas Connell, Basil
Robert Ward und Colin Anderson
Lucas, 1937**
Wohnhaus in Wentworth, Surrey,
Eingangsseite
House in Wentworth, Surrey.
Entrance side
Immeuble d'habitation à Went-
worth, Surrey, côté de l'entrée

**Amyas Douglas Connell, Basil
Robert Ward und Colin Anderson
Lucas, 1937**
Wohnhaus in Wentworth, Surrey,
Gartenseite
House in Wentworth, Surrey.
Garden side
Immeuble d'habitation à Went-
worth, Surrey, côté jardin

**Amyas Douglas Connell, Basil
Robert Ward und Colin Anderson
Lucas, 1938**
Wohnhaus in Frognal, Hampstead,
London, Gartenseite
House at Frognal, Hampstead,
London, View from garden
Immeuble d'habitation à Frognal,
Hampstead, Londres, côté jardin

**Amyas Douglas Connell, Basil
Robert Ward und Colin Anderson
Lucas, 1938**
Wohnhaus in Frognal, Hampstead,
London, Straßenseite
House at Frognal, Hampstead,
London, View from road
Immeuble d'habitation à Frognal,
Hampstead, Londres, côté rue

Joseph Emberton, 1932
Yachtklub »Royal Corinthian« in
Burnham-on-Crouch, Essex
Royal Corinthian Yacht Club,
Burnham-on-Crouch, Essex
Yachtclub »Royal Corinthian« à
Burnham-on-Crouch, Essex

Edwin Maxwell Fry, 1937
Villa »Miramonte« in Kingston, Sur-
rey, Gartenseite
»Miramonte« in Kingston, Surrey.
View from the garden
Villa »Miramonte« à Kingston, Sur-
rey, côté jardin

Edwin Maxwell Fry, 1936
Wohnhaus in Hampstead, London,
Straßenseite
House at Hampstead, London.
View from the road
Immeuble d'habitation à Hamp-
stead, Londres, côté rue

Edwin Maxwell Fry, 1938
Mietwohnhaus in London
Flats in London
Immeuble à Londres

Edwin Maxwell Fry, 1936
Werkswohnungsanlage »Kensal
House« der Gaswerke in London,
Westseite
»Kensal House«. Workers' accom-
modation of the London gasworks.
West view
Complexe d'appartements de fonc-
tions »Kensal House« des usines à
gaz de Londres, côté ouest

Denys Lasdun, 1938
Wohnung und Atelier eines Malers
in London
Artist's flat and studio in London
Appartement et atelier d'un peintre
à Londres

Frederick Gibberd, 1934
Wohnanlage »Pullman Court« in
Streatham, London, Eingang und
Treppenhaus
»Pullman Court« residential
development in Streatham, London.
Entrance and staircase
Complexe d'habitation »Pullman
Court« à Streatham, Londres,
entrée et cage d'escalier

Raymond McGrath, 1936
Villa St. Ann's Hill in Chertsey,
Surrey, Nordseite
St. Ann's Hill villa in Chertsey,
Surrey. North view
Villa St. Ann's Hill à Chertsey,
Surrey, côté nord

Raymond McGrath, 1936
Villa St. Ann's Hill in Chertsey,
Surrey, Gartenseite
St. Ann's Hill villa in Chertsey,
Surrey. View from the garden
Villa St. Ann's Hill à Chertsey,
Surrey, côté jardin

Raymond McGrath, 1936
Villa St. Ann's Hill in Chertsey,
Surrey, Terrasse
St. Ann's Hill villa in Chertsey,
Surrey. Terrace
Villa St. Ann's Hill à Chertsey,
Surrey, terrasse

**Francis Reginald Stevens Yorke,
1935**
Villa in Nast Hyde, Hatfield, Hert-
fordshire, Ansicht von Südwesten
Villa at Nast Hyde, Hatfield, Hert-
fordshire. South-west view
Villa à Nast Hyde, Hatfield, Hert-
fordshire, vue du sud-ouest

**Francis Reginald Stevens Yorke,
1935**
Villa in Nast Hyde, Hatfield, Hert-
fordshire, Ansicht von Nordosten
Villa at Nast Hyde, Hatfield, Hert-
fordshire. North-east view
Villa à Nast Hyde, Hatfield, Hert-
fordshire, vue du nord-est

Thomas S. Tait
Haus in Silverend
House at Silverend
Maison à Silverend

**Francis Reginald Stevens Yorke und
Marcel Breuer, 1937**
Villa in Angmering-on-Sea, Sussex,
Ansicht von Südwesten
Villa in Angmering-on-Sea, Sussex.
South-west view
Villa à Angmering-on-Sea, Sussex,
vue du sud-ouest

IRAN

Gabriel Guevrekian, 1936
Villa Ch. Kosrovani in Teheran,
Gartenseite
The Ch. Kosrovani Villa in Teheran.
View from the garden
Villa Ch. Kosrovani à Téhéran, côté
jardin

I S R A E L

Joseph Neufeld, 1932–1935
Kinderheim in Mishmar Haemek,
Haifa, Westseite
Children's home in Mishmar
Haemek, Haifa. West view
Foyer d'enfants à Mishmar Hae-
mek, Haifa, côté jardin

Joseph Neufeld, 1932–1935
Kinderheim in Mishmar Haemek,
Haifa, Morgenterrasse
Children's home in Mishmar
Haemek, Haifa. Morning terrace
Foyer d'enfants à Mishmar Hae-
mek, Haifa, terrasse du matin

Joseph Neufeld, 1936
Arbeitersiedlung in Tel Aviv, Hofseite
Workers' estate in Tel Aviv. View
from the courtyard
Habitat d'ouvriers à Tel Aviv, côté
cour

Joseph Neufeld, 1936
Arbeitersiedlung in Darom, Tel
Aviv, Westseite
Workers' estate in Darom, Tel Aviv.
West view
Habitat d'ouvriers à Darom, Tel
Aviv, côté ouest

Joseph Neufeld, 1935
Privatklinik in Tel Aviv, Ansicht des
Operationsbaus
Private clinic in Tel Aviv. View of the
operating-theatre building
Clinique privée à Tel Aviv, vue du
bâtiment d'opération

Joseph Neufeld, 1935
Privatklinik in Tel Aviv, links die
Isolierstation
Private clinic in Tel Aviv. On the left,
the isolation ward
Clinique privée à Tel Aviv, à
gauche la station d'isolement

Joseph Neufeld, 1935
Privatklinik in Tel Aviv, Ansicht von
Westen
Private clinic in Tel Aviv. View from
the west
Clinique privée à Tel Aviv, vue de
l'ouest

Joseph Neufeld, 1935
Privatklinik in Tel Aviv, Hauptgebäude
Private clinic in Tel Aviv. Main
building
Clinique privée à Tel Aviv, bâtiment
principal

Joseph Neufeld, 1935
Villa G. in Tel-Benyamin, Tel Aviv,
Gartenseite
Villa G. in Tel-Benyamin, Tel Aviv.
View from the garden
Villa G. à Tel-Benyamin, Tel Aviv,
côté jardin

ITALIEN

Franco Albini, Renato Camus und Giancarlo Palanti, 1936–1938
Siedlung »Fabio Filzi« in Mailand, Hofseite
»Fabio Filzi« estate in Milan. View from the courtyard
Lotissement »Fabio Filzi« à Milan, côté cour

**Franco Albini, Renato Camus und
Giancarlo Palanti, 1936–1938**
Siedlung »Fabio Filzi« in Mailand,
Gesamtansicht; Grundriß dreier
Wohneinheiten
»Fabio Filzi« estate in Milan. Over-
all view; plan for three units of
accommodation
Lotissement »Fabio Filzi« à Milan,
vue d'ensemble; plan de trois unités
d'habitation

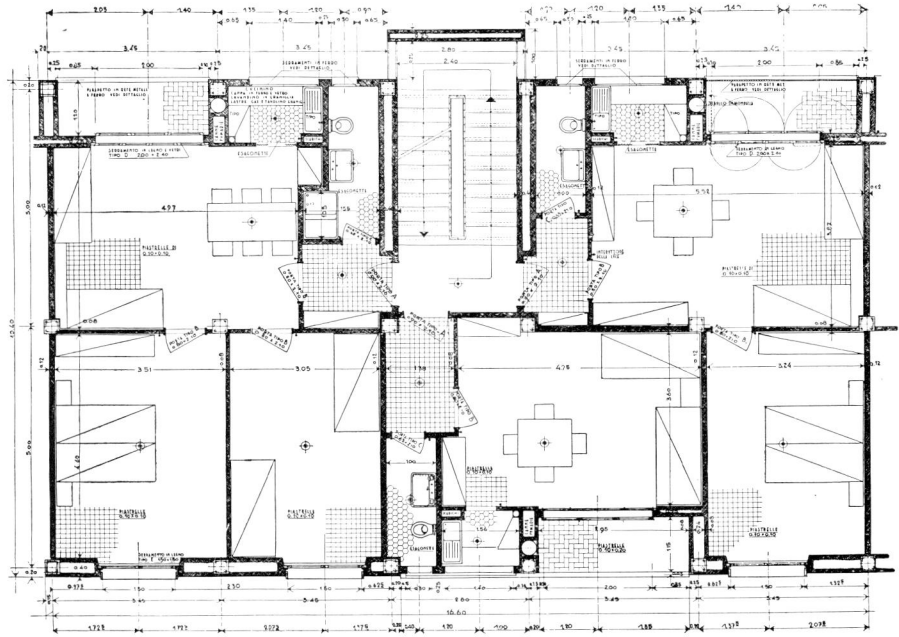

Gianni Angelini, Pepp. Calderara und Tito Varisco Bassanesi, 1938–1939
Sitz der faschistischen Stadtteilgruppe »Pietro Edoardo Crespi« in Mailand, Ansicht und Erdgeschoßgrundriß
Headquarters of the local faschist group »Pietro Edoardo Crespi« in Milan. View and ground-floor plan
Siège du groupe fasciste de quartier »Pietro Edoardo Crespi« à Milan, vue de face et plan du rez-de-chaussée

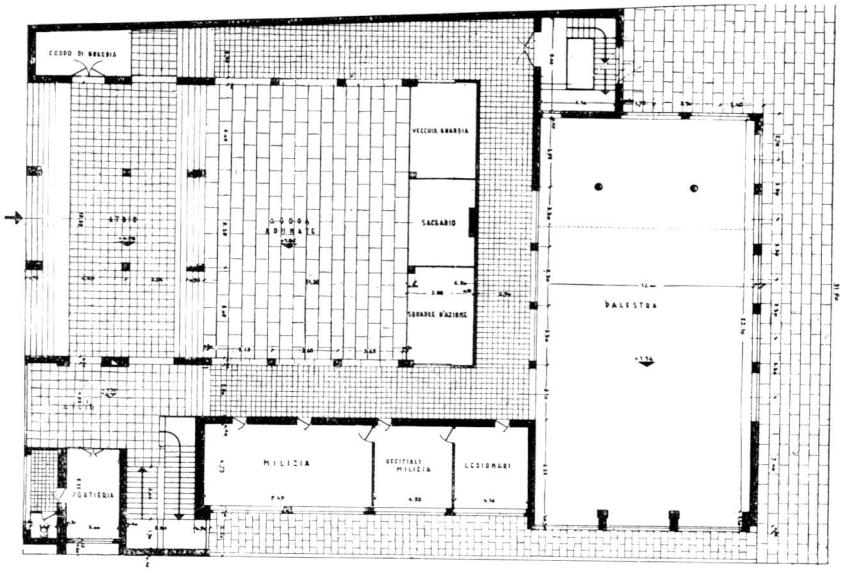

**Alberico Barbiano di Belgiojoso,
G. L. Banfi, L. B. di Belgiojoso,
E. Peressutti und E. N. Rogers**
Haus Feltrinelli in Mailand
The Feltrinelli house in Milan
Maison Feltrinelli à Milan

**Gian Luigi Banfi, Lodovico Bar-
biano di Belgiojoso, Enrico Peres-
sutti und Ernesto N. Rogers,
1937–1938**
Sonnentherapiezentrum in Legnano
Sun therapy centre in Legnano
Centre de thérapie solaire à
Legnano

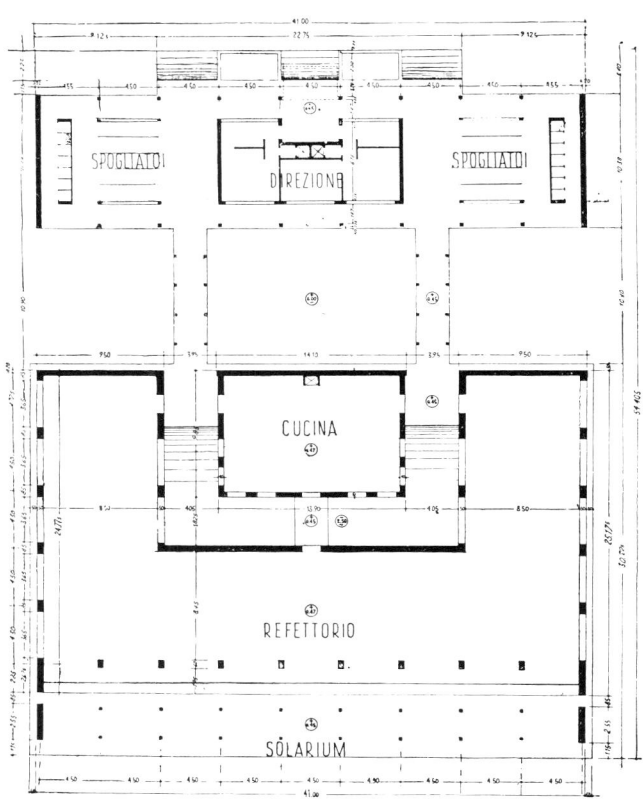

Gian Luigi Banfi, Lodovico Barbiano di Belgiojoso, Enrico Peressutti und Ernesto N. Rogers, 1937–1938
Sonnentherapiezentrum in Legnano, links Umkleide- und Büroräume, rechts Küche und Speisesaal; Grundriß
Sun therapy centre in Legnano. Changing rooms and offices (left), kitchen and dining room (right); ground plan
Centre de thérapie solaire à Legnano, à gauche les vestiaires et bureaux, à droite la cuisine et la salle à manger; plan

Piero Bottoni und Mario Pucci, 1940
Reithalle der »Gioventù Italiana del
Littorio« in Bologna, Innenansicht
mit Blick auf die Tribüne
Indoor riding accommodation of
»Gioventù Italiana del Littorio« in
Bologna. Interior view showing the
grandstand
Centre d'équitation de la »Gioventù
Italiana del Littorio« à Bologne, vue
intérieure avec vue sur les tribunes

Piero Bottoni und Mario Pucci, 1940
Reithalle der »Gioventù Italiana del
Littorio« in Bologna
Indoor riding accommodation of
»Gioventù Italiana del Littorio« in
Bologna
Centre d'équitation de la »Gioventù
Italiana del Littorio« à Bologne

Piero Bottoni und Mario Pucci, 1939
Fabrikgebäude in Bologna
Factory building in Bologna
Bâtiment d'usine à Bologne

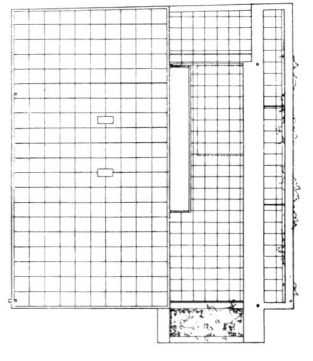

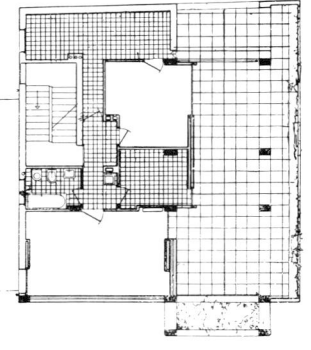

Cesare Cattaneo, 1938–1939
Mietwohnhaus in Cernobbio,
Como, Ansicht von Süden; Grundrisse der vier Geschosse
Flats in Cernobbio, Como. View
from the south; plan of the four
floors
Immeuble à Cernobbio, Côme, vue
du sud; plans des quatre étages

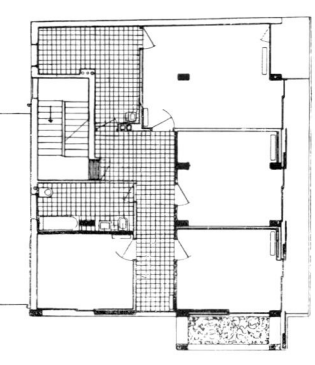

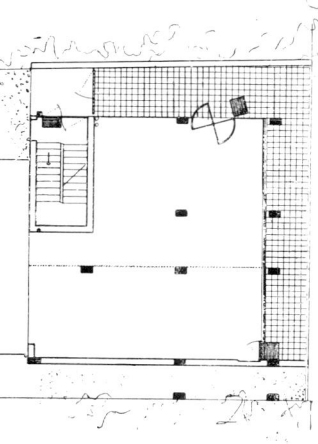

Cesare Cattaneo, 1938–1939
Mietwohnhaus in Cernobbio,
Como, Ansicht von Südwesten
Flats in Cernobbio, Como. View
from the south-west
Immeuble à Cernobbio, Côme, vue
du sud-ouest

Cesare Cattaneo, 1935–1937
Kindergarten »Giuseppe Garbagnati« in Asnago, Como, Eingangsseite
»Giuseppe Garbagnati« kindergarten in Asagno, Como. Entrance
side
Jardin d'enfants »Giuseppe Garbagnati« à Asnago, Côme, côté de
l'entrée

Cesare Cattaneo, 1935–1937
Kindergarten »Giuseppe Garbagnati« in Asnago, Como, Rückseite
mit Aula
»Giuseppe Garbagnati« kindergarten in Asagno, Como. Rear view
showing assembly hall
Jardin d'enfants »Giuseppe Garbagnati« à Asnago, Côme, côté
postérieur avec salle des fêtes

Mario Cereghini, 1934–1935
»Casa Madre« der »Gioventù
Italiana del Littorio« in Mailand,
Straßenansicht
The »Casa Madre« of the
»Gioventù Italiano del Littorio« in
Milan. View from the road
»Casa Madre« de la »Gioventù Ita-
liana del Littorio« à Milan, façade
donnant sur la rue

Mario Cereghini, 1934–1935
»Casa Madre« der »Gioventù
Italiana del Littorio« in Mailand,
Aufgang zur Bibliothek
The »Casa Madre« of the
»Gioventù Italiano del Littorio« in
Milan. The stairs to the library
»Casa Madre« de la »Gioventù Ita-
liana del Littorio« à Milan, escalier
sur la bibliothèque

Gaetano Ciocca, 1939
Landarbeiterhäuser aus vorgefer-
tigten Elementen in Merone/Lecco
Prefabricated farm-workers'
houses in Merone, Lecco
Maisons d'agriculteurs composées
d'éléments préfabriqués à Merone/
Lecco

Luigi Carlo Daneri, 1934–1940
Wohnhochhaus in Genua, vom
Strand gesehen
Multistorey flats in Genoa. View
from the beach
Tour d'habitation à Gênes, vue de
la plage

Luigi Carlo Daneri, 1934–1940
Wohnhochhaus in Genua
Multistorey flats in Genoa
Tour d'habitation à Gênes

Luigi Carlo Daneri, 1938–1939
Ferienkolonie »Senatore Rinaldo
Piaggio« in S. Stefano d'Aveto
»Senatore Rinaldo Piaggio« holi-
day camp in S. Stefano d'Aveto
Colonie de vacances »Senatore
Rinaldo Piaggio« à S. Stefano
d'Aveto

Luigi Carlo Daneri, 1938–1939
Ferienkolonie »Senatore Rinaldo
Piaggio« in S. Stefano d'Aveto,
Ansicht von der Zufahrt; Speisesaal
»Senatore Rinaldo Piaggio« holi-
day camp in S. Stefano d'Aveto.
View of driveway. Dining hall
Colonie de vacances »Senatore
Rinaldo Piaggio« à S. Stefano
d'Aveto, vue de la voie d'accès;
réfectoire

**Augusto Magnaghi Delfino und
Mario Terzaghi, 1939**
Wohnhaus in Fino Mornasco,
Como, Straßenseite
Flats in Fino Mornasco, Como.
View from the road
Immeuble à Fino Mornasco, Côme,
côté rue

**Augusto Magnaghi Delfino und
Mario Terzaghi, 1939**
Wohnhaus in Fino Mornasco,
Como, offenes Treppenhaus
Flats in Fino Mornasco, Como.
Open stairwell
Immeuble à Fino Mornasco, Côme,
cage d'escalier ouverte

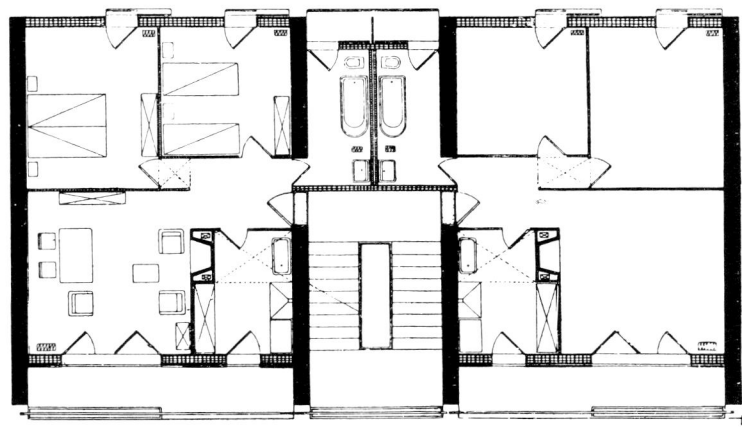

**Augusto Magnaghi Delfino und
Mario Terzaghi, 1939**
Wohnhaus in Fino Mornasco
Como, Nordseite; Grundriß zweier
Wohneinheiten
Flats in Fino Mornasco, Como.
North side; ground plan of two flats
Immeuble à Fino Mornasco, Côme,
côté nord; plan de deux logements

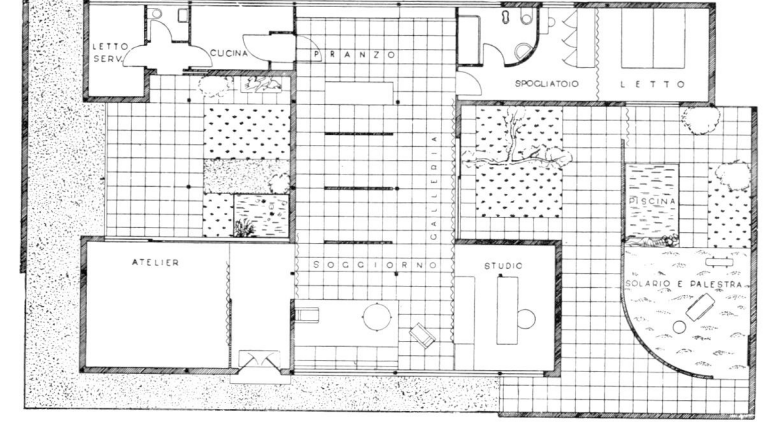

Luigi Figini und Gino Pollini, 1933
Atelierhaus für einen Künstler,
gezeigt auf der Triennale in Mailand, Blick aus dem Atelier in den
Innenhof; Grundriß
Painter's studio house, shown at the
Triennale in Milan. View from the
studio over the interior courtyard;
ground plan
Maison atelier pour un artiste, pré-
sentée à la Triennale de Milan, vue
à partir de l'atelier sur la cour intérieure; plan

Luigi Figini und Gino Pollini, 1933
Atelierhaus für einen Künstler,
gezeigt auf der Triennale in Mailand, Freiplatz mit Bassin; Eingangsseite
Painter's studio house, shown at the
Triennale in Milan. Open-air area
with pond. Entrance side
Maison atelier pour un artiste, pré-
sentée à la Triennale de Milan,
place en plein air et bassin; côté de
l'éntrée

Luigi Figini, 1934–1935
Haus des Architekten im »Dorf der
Journalisten« in Mailand, Patio
neben dem Eßzimmer; Ostfassade
The architect's house in the
»Journalists' Village« in Milan.
Patio beside the dining room. East
facade
Maison de l'architecte dans le »Vil-
lage des journalistes« à Milan,
patio à côté de la salle à manger;
façade est

Luigi Figini, 1934–1935
Haus des Architekten im »Dorf der
Journalisten« in Mailand, Eßzimmer; Grundrisse der beiden Wohn-
geschosse
The architect's house in the »Journalists' Village« in Milan. Dining
room; ground plan for the two residential floors
Maison de l'architecte dans le »Village des journalistes« à Milan,
salle à manger; plans des deux
étages d'habitation

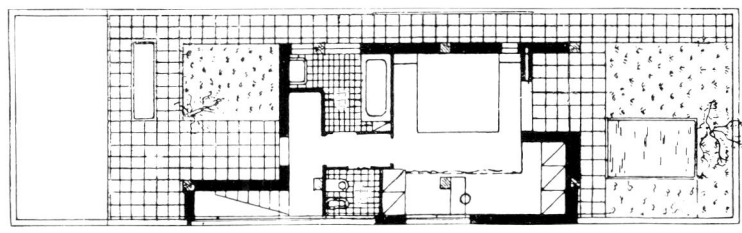

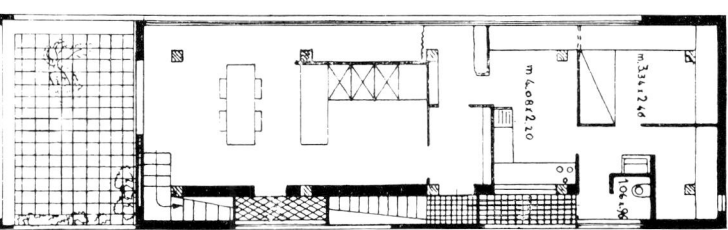

**Luigi Baldessari, Luigi Figini und
Gino Pollini, 1931–1932**
Verwaltungsbau der Firma De
Angeli Frua in Mailand
Administration building of the De
Angeli Frua company in Milan
Immeuble administratif de l'entre-
prise De Angeli Frua à Milan

Luigi Figini und Gino Pollini, 1937
Bürogebäude der Firma Olivetti in
Ivrea, Treppenhaus
Office building of the Olivetti
company in Ivrea. Staircase
Bâtiment de bureaux de l'entreprise
Olivetti à Ivrea, cage d'escalier

**Ignazio Gardella und Luigi Martini,
1935–1938**
Lungentherapiezentrum in Alessan-
dria, Ansichten
Lung therapy centre in Alessandria.
Views
Centre de thérapie pulmonaire à
Arlessandria, vues

Gian Luigi Giordani, 1938
Flughafen Forlanini, Mailand-
Linate, Ansicht vom Rollfeld
Forlanini airport, Linate, Milan.
View from the runway
Aéroport Forlanini, Milan-Linate,
vue de la piste d'atterrissage

Gian Luigi Giordani, 1938
Flughafen Forlanini, Mailand-
Linate, Dienstgebäude
Forlanini airport, Linate, Milan.
Service building
Aéroport Forlanini, Milan-Linate,
bâtiments de service

Enrico A. Griffini und Cesare Fratino, 1937–1938
Kindererholungsheim »Lino Redaelli« in Cesenatico, Seeseite; Fassadendetail
The »Lino Redaelli« children's convalescent home in Cesenatico. View from the sea. Detail of the facade
Maison de santé pour enfants »Lino Redaelli« à Cesenatico, côté mer; détail de la façade

Mario Labò, 1937
Restaurant »San Pietro« in Genua
(oben)
Restaurant »San Pietro« in Genoa
(above)
Restaurant »San Pietro« à Gênes
(en haut)

Mario Labò, 1940
Wohnhaus in Genua (unten)
Flats in Genoa (below)
Immeuble à Gênes (en bas)

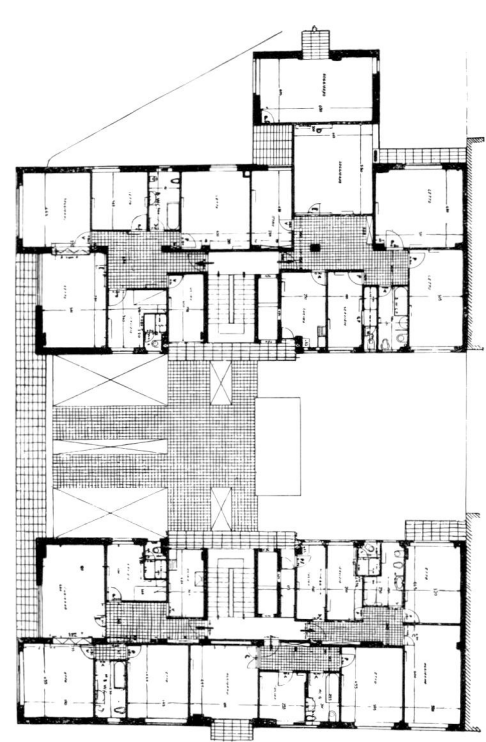

**Pietro Lingeri und Giuseppe
Terragni, 1934–1935**
»Casa Rustici« in Mailand, Straßenseite; Grundriß einer Wohnetage
»Casa Rustici« in Milan. View from
the road. Ground plan of a residential storey
»Casa Rustici« à Milan, côté rue;
plan d'un étage d'habitation

**Pietro Lingeri und Giuseppe
Terragni, 1934–1935**
»Casa Lavezzari« in Mailand
»Casa Lavezzari« in Milan
»Casa Lavezzari« à Milan

Pietro Lingeri, 1935–1939
Atelierhaus auf der Insel Comacina
im Comer See, Frontansicht
Studio house on the island of
Comacina on Lake Como. Front
view
Maison atelier sur l'île Comacina
sur le lac de Côme, vue de face

Pietro Lingeri, 1935–1939
Atelierhaus auf der Insel Comacina
im Comer See, Seitenansicht
Studio house on the island of
Comacina on Lake Como. Side
view
Maison atelier sur l'île Comacina
sur le lac de Côme, vue de côté

Pietro Lingeri, 1930
Yachtklub »Amila« in Tremezzo am
Comer See
»Amila« yacht club in Tremezzo on
Lake Como
Yachtclub »Amila« à Tremezzo au
bord du lac de Côme

Pietro Lingeri, 1930
Yachtklub »Amila« in Tremezzo am
Comer See, Straßenseite
»Amila« yacht club in Tremezzo on
Lake Como. View from the road
Yachtclub »Amila« à Tremezzo au
bord du lac de Côme, côté rue

Pietro Lingeri, 1935–1936
Haus in Como
House in Como
Maison à Côme

**Camillo Magni, Sandro Pasquali
und Bino Opoczynski, 1938**
Villa Malvicini in Mailand, Gartenterrasse
The Malvicini Villa in Milan. Garden terrace
Villa Malvicini à Milan, terrasse
jardin

Pier Luigi Nervi, 1930–1932
Stadion »Giovanni Berta« in
Florenz, Haupttribüne
The »Giovanni Berta« stadium in
Florence. The main grandstand
Stade »Giovanni Berta« à Florence,
tribune principale

Pier Luigi Nervi, 1930–1932
Stadion »Giovanni Berta« in
Florenz, Aufgang zur Tribüne
The »Giovanni Berta« stadium in
Florence. Stairs to the grandstand
Stade »Giovanni Berta« à Florence,
montée vers la tribune

Pier Luigi Nervi, 1938
Flugzeughangar in Orbetello,
Stütze mit Führung der Schiebetore
Aircraft hangar in Orbetello.
Support with guide for sliding doors
Hangar d'avion à Orbetello, appui
avec rail des portails coulissants

Pier Luigi Nervi, 1938
Flugzeughangar in Orbetello,
Gesamtansicht
Aircraft hangar in Orbetello.
Overall view
Hangar d'avion à Orbetello, vue
d'ensemble

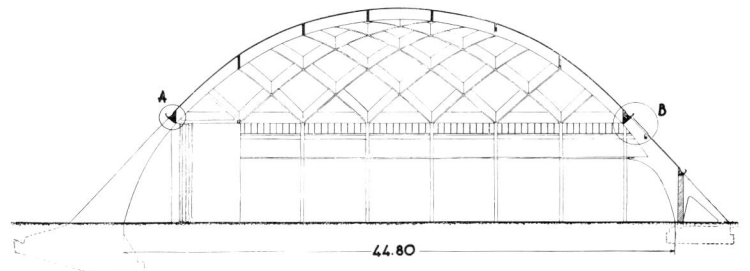

Pier Luigi Nervi, 1938
Flugzeughangar in Orbetello,
Ansicht und Zeichnungen der Stahl-
betonkonstruktion
Aircraft hangar in Orbetello. View
and drawings of the reinforced
concrete construction
Hangar d'avion à Orbetello, vue et
dessins de la construction en béton
armé

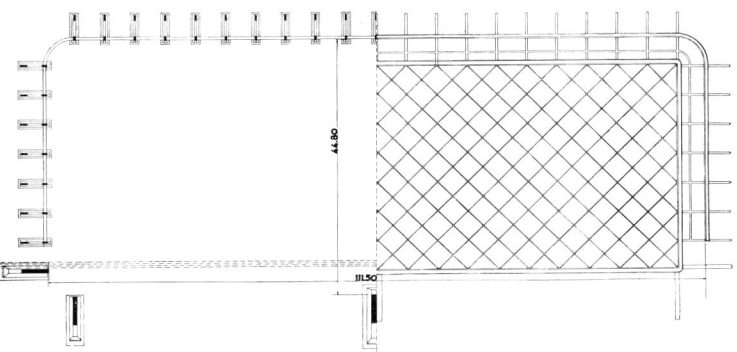

Giuseppe Pagano, 1936
Erweiterung des Palazzo dell'Arte
in Mailand, Ausstellungsraum mit
Wendeltreppe
Extension of the Palazzo dell'Arte in
Milan. Exhibition room with spiral
staircase
Agrandissement du Palazzo del-
l'Arte à Milan, salle d'exposition
avec escalier en colimaçon

Giuseppe Pagano, 1936
Erweiterung des Palazzo dell'Arte
in Mailand
Extension of the Palazzo dell'Arte in
Milan
Agrandissement du Palazzo del-
l'Arte à Milan

Giuseppe Pagano, 1936
Erweiterung des Palazzo dell'Arte
in Mailand, Verbindung zum Altbau
Extension of the Palazzo dell'Arte in
Milan. Connection with the old
building
Agrandissement du Palazzo del-
l'Arte à Milan, lien avec l'ancien
bâtiment

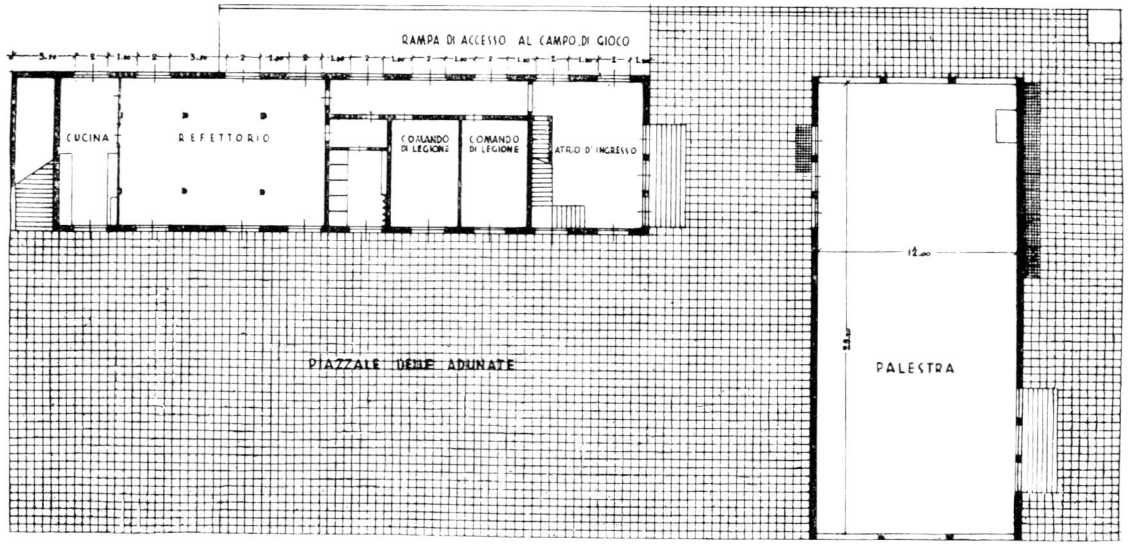

Agnoldomenico Pica, 1937–1939
Haus der »Gioventù Italiana del Littorio« in Narni, Eingangsbereich; Grundriß
House of the »Gioventù Italiana del Littorio« in Narni. Entrance area; ground plan
Maison de »Gioventú Italiana del Littorio« à Narni, zone de l'entrée; plan

RAMPA DI ACCESSO AL CAMPO DI GIOCO

CUCINA REFETTORIO COMANDO DI LEGIONE COMANDO DI LEGIONE ATRIO D'INGRESSO

PIAZZALE DELLE ADUNATE

PALESTRA

Agnoldomenico Pica, 1937–1939
Haus der »Gioventù Italiana del Littorio« in Narni, Ansicht von Süden
House of the »Gioventù Italiana del Littorio« in Narni. View from the south
Maison de »Gioventù Italiana del Littorio« à Narni, vue du sud

Agnoldomenico Pica, 1937–1939
Haus der »Gioventù Italiana del Littorio« in Narni, Ansicht von Westen
House of the »Gioventú Italiana del Littorio« in Narni. View from the west
Maison de »Gioventù Italiana del Littorio« à Narni, vue de l'ouest

Gio Ponti, Antonio Fornaroli und Eugenio Soncini, 1935–1938
Verwaltungsgebäude der Montecatini-Gruppe in Mailand, Rohrpostzentrale
Administration building of the Montecatini Group in Milan. Pneumatic postage centre
Bâtiment administratif du groupe Montecatini à Milan, centrale de poste pneumatique

**Gio Ponti, Antonio Fornaroli und
Eugenio Soncini, 1935–1938**
Verwaltungsgebäude der Montecatini-Gruppe in Mailand, Hofseite
Administration building of the
Montecatini Group in Milan. View
from courtyard
Bâtiment administratif du groupe
Montecatini à Milan, côté cour

Enrico Prampolini, 1933
Flugplatzgebäude, gezeigt auf der
Triennale in Mailand
Airport building, shown at the
Triennale in Milan
Bâtiment de l'aérodrome, présenté
à la Triennale à Milan

Mario Ridolfi, 1936–1937
Wohnhaus in Rom
Flats in Rome
Immeuble à Rome

Mario Ridolfi, 1936–1937
Wohnhaus in Rom, Grundriß einer
Wohnetage
Flats in Rome. Ground plan of
accommodation floor
Immeuble à Rome, plan d'un étage
d'habitation

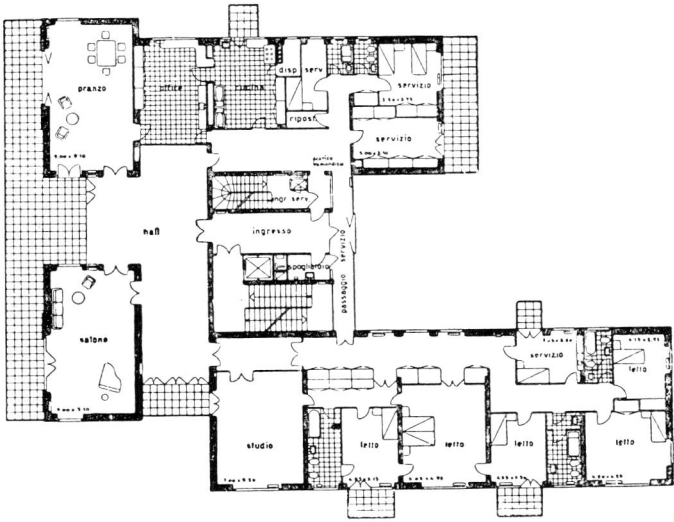

Giuseppe Terragni, 1932–1936
Casa del Fascio in Como, südliche
Ecke
Casa del Fascio in Como. South
corner
Casa del Fascio à Côme, angle sud

Giuseppe Terragni, 1932–1936
Casa del Fascio in Como, Fassade
zur Piazza dell'Impero
Casa del Fascio in Como. Facade
on the Piazza dell'Impero
Casa del Fascio à Côme, façade
donnant sur la Piazza dell'Impero

Giuseppe Terragni, 1932–1936
Casa del Fascio in Como, Nord-
westseite
Casa del Fascio in Como. View
from the north-west
Casa del Fascio à Côme, côté nord-
ouest

Giuseppe Terragni, 1932–1936
Casa del Fascio in Como, östliche
Ecke
Casa del Fascio in Como. East
corner
Casa del Fascio à Côme, angle est

Giuseppe Terragni, 1932–1936
Casa del Fascio in Como, Neben-
eingänge an der Nordostseite
Casa del Fascio in Como. Side
entrance on the north-east side
Casa del Fascio à Côme, entrées
secondaires du côté nord-est

Giuseppe Terragni, 1932–1936
Casa del Fascio in Como, Sitzungs-
saal
Casa del Fascio in Como.
Conference hall
Casa del Fascio à Côme, salle de
réunion

Giuseppe Terragni, 1932–1936
Casa del Fascio in Como, Treppen-
aufgang
Casa del Fascio in Como. Staircase
Casa del Fascio à Côme, montée
d'escalier

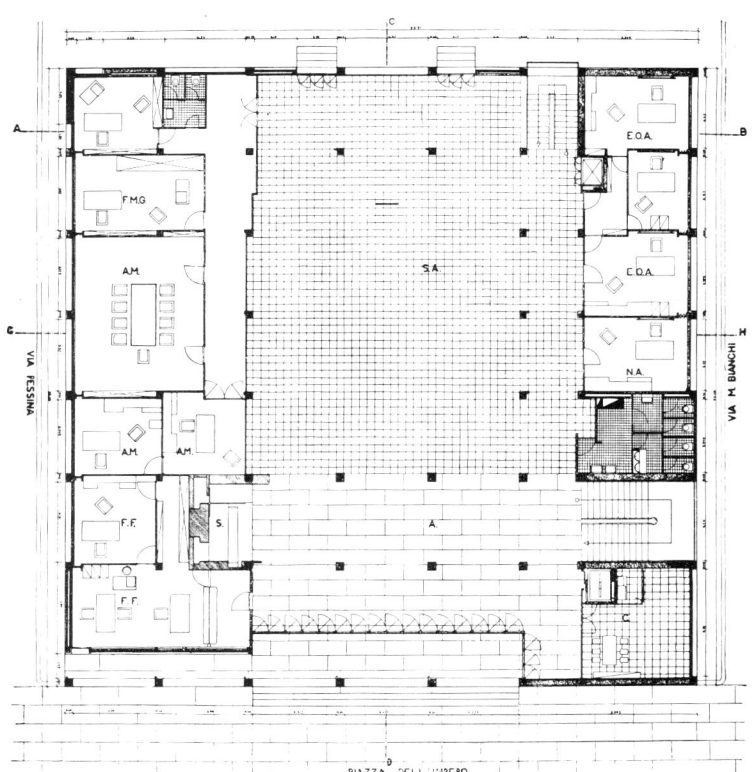

Giuseppe Terragni, 1932–1936
Casa del Fascio in Como, Haupteingang mit 18 Türflügeln, die sich
simultan öffnen und schließen; Erdgeschoßgrundriß
Casa del Fascio in Como. Main
entrance with eighteen door panels
which open and close simultan-
eously; ground-floor plan
Casa del Fascio à Côme, entrée
principale avec 18 battants de
portes qui s'ouvrent et se ferment
simultanément; plan du rez-de-
chaussée

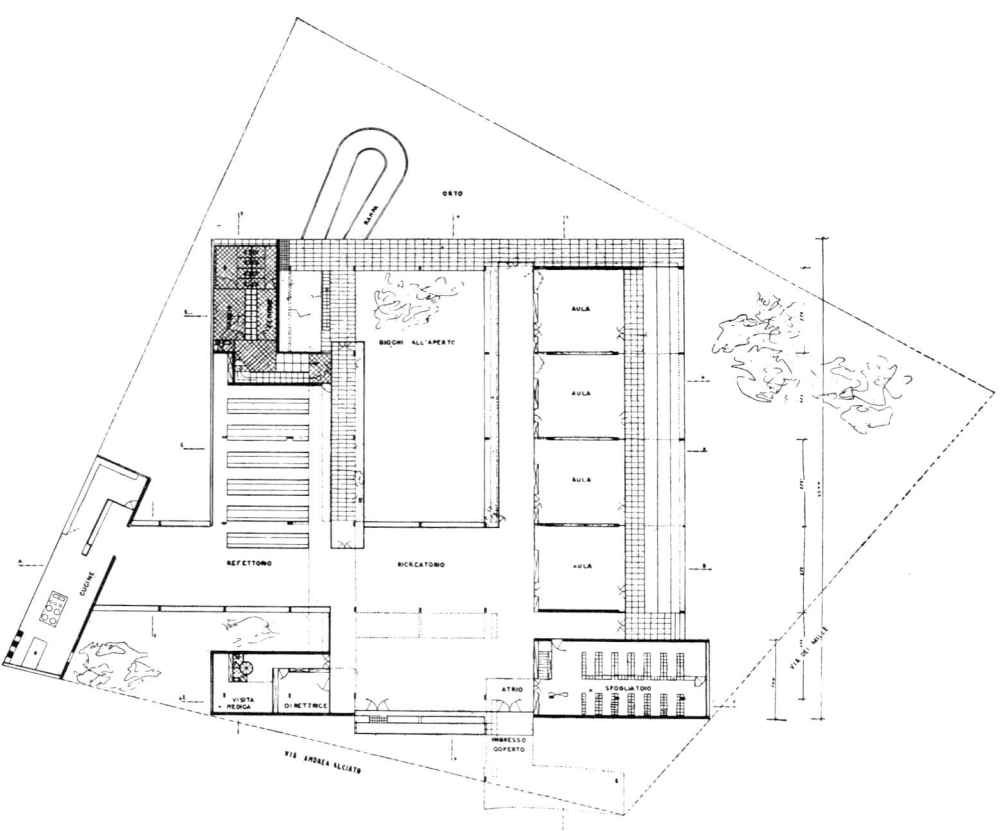

Giuseppe Terragni, 1932—1937
Kindergarten »Antonio Sant'Elia« in
Como, Glasfront der Gruppen-
räume; Grundriß
»Antonio Sant'Elia« kindergarten in
Como. Glass frontage to the group
rooms; ground plan
Jardin d'enfants »Antonio Sant'E-
lia« à Côme, façade vitrée des
salles de groupe; plan

Giuseppe Terragni, 1932–1937
Kindergarten »Antonio Sant'Elia« in
Como, Glasfront der Gruppenräume mit aufgespannten Sonnen-
segeln
»Antonio Sant'Elia« kindergarten in
Como. Glass frontage to the group
rooms with sun-sails opened
Jardin d'enfants »Antonio Sant'E-
lia« à Côme, façade vitrée des
salles de groupe avec voiles de
soleil déployées

Giuseppe Terragni, 1932–1937
Kindergarten »Antonio Sant'Elia« in
Como, Innenhof
»Antonio Sant'Elia« kindergarten in
Como. Inner courtyard
Jardin d'enfants »Antonio Sant'E-
lia« à Côme, cour intérieure

Giuseppe Terragni, 1932–1937
Kindergarten »Antonio Sant'Elia« in
Como, Straßenseite
»Antonio Sant'Elia« kindergarten in
Como. View from the road
Jardin d'enfants »Antonio Sant'E-
lia« à Côme, côté rue

Giuseppe Terragni, 1932–1937
Kindergarten »Antonio Sant'Elia« in
Como, Haupteingang
»Antonio Sant'Elia« kindergarten in
Como. Main entrance
Jardin d'enfants »Antonio Sant'E-
lia« à Côme, entrée principale

Giuseppe Terragni, 1932–1937
Kindergarten »Antonio Sant'Elia« in
Como, Gruppenräume mit geöffne-
ten Trennwänden
»Antonio Sant'Elia« kindergarten in
Como. Group rooms with partitions
open
Jardin d'enfants »Antonio Sant'E-
lia« à Côme, salles de groupe avec
cloisons de séparation ouvertes

Giuseppe Terragni, 1939–1940
Appartementhaus Giuliani-Frigerio
in Como, Ostseite
Giuliani Frigerio apartment building in Como. View from the east
Immeuble de studios Giuliani-Frigerio à Côme, côté est

Giuseppe Terragni, 1939–1940
Appartementhaus Giuliani-Frigerio
in Como, Nordseite
Giuliani Frigerio apartment building in Como. View from the north
Immeuble de studios Giuliani-Frigerio à Côme, côté nord

Giuseppe Terragni, 1936–1937
Villa Bianca in Seveso, Como, Gartenseite
Villa Bianca in Seveso, Como. View from the garden
Villa Bianca à Seveso, Côme, côté jardin

Giuseppe Terragni und Antonio Carminati, 1938–1939
Casa del Fascio in Lissone, Fassade zum Platz
Casa del Fascio in Lissone. Facade on the square
Casa del Fascio à Lissone, façade donnant sur la place

Giuseppe Terragni und Antonio Carminati, 1938–1939
Casa del Fascio in Lissone, Notausgänge des Saals
Casa del Fascio in Lissone. Emergency exits from the hall
Casa del Fascio à Lissone, sorties de secours de la salle

**Giuseppe Terragni und Antonio
Carminati, 1938–1939**
Casa del Fascio in Lissone, Trep-
penhaus im ersten Stock; Grundriß
Casa del Fascio in Lissone. First-
floor staircase; ground plan
Casa del Fascio à Lissone, cage
d'escalier au premier étage; plan

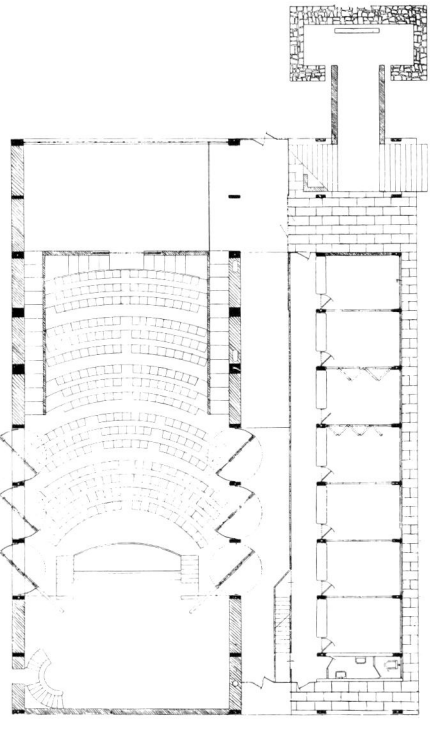

Giuseppe Vaccaro, 1938
Ferienkolonie der Firma AGIP in
Cesenatico, Straßenseite des
Schlaftrakts
Holiday camp of the AGIP com‑
pany in Cesenatico. Dormitory wing
seen from the road
Colonie de vacances de l'entreprise
AGIP à Cesenatico, côté rue de
l'aile du dortoir

Giuseppe Vaccaro, 1938
Ferienkolonie der Firma AGIP in
Cesenatico, Eingangsbereich mit
Blick auf Speisesaal und Meer
Holiday camp of the AGIP com‑
pany in Cesenatico. Entrance area
with view of the dining hall and the
sea
Colonie de vacances de l'entreprise
AGIP à Cesenatico, zone de l'en‑
trée avec vue sur le réfectoire et sur
la mer

Giuseppe Vaccaro, 1938
Ferienkolonie der Firma AGIP in
Cesenatico, vom Strand aus gese‑
hen
Holiday camp of the AGIP com‑
pany in Cesenatico. View from the
beach
Colonie de vacances de l'entreprise
AGIP à Cesenatico, vue de la plage

J A P A N

Bauamt der Stadt Tokio, 1933
Grundschule »Yotsuya« in Tokio,
Südseite
»Yotsuya« elementary school in
Tokyo. South view
Ecole primaire »Yotsuya« à Tokyo,
côté sud

Bauamt der Stadt Tokio, 1933
Grundschule »Yotsuya« in Tokio,
Treppenturm
»Yotsuya« elementary school in
Tokyo. Stairwell tower
Ecole primaire »Yotsuya« à Tokyo,
tour de l'escalier

Bauamt der Stadt Tokio, 1933
Grundschule »Tsukudo« in Tokio,
Gesamtansicht
»Tsukudo« elementary school in
Tokyo. Overall view
Ecole primaire »Tsukudo« à Tokyo,
vue d'ensemble

Kameki Tsuchiura, 1933
Villa H. Yamamoto in Tokio, Süd-
seite
The H. Yamamota villa in Tokyo.
South view
Villa H. Yamamoto à Tokyo, côté
sud

Bunzo Yamaguchi, 1934
Dentistenschule in Tokio
Dentists' school in Tokyo
Ecole de médecine dentaire à
Tokyo

Bunzo Yamaguchi, 1934
Dentistenschule in Tokio, Zufahrt
Dentists' school in Tokyo. Driveway
Ecole de médecine dentaire à
Tokyo, voie d'accès

Bunzo Yamaguchi, 1934
Dentistenschule in Tokio, Eingangs-
bereich
Dentists' school in Tokyo. Entrance
area
Ecole de médecine dentaire à
Tokyo, zone de l'entrée

LIBYEN

Giovanni Pellegrini, 1934
Villa Salvi in Tripolis, Eingang und
Pergola
The Salvi villa in Tripoli. Entrance
and pergola
Villa Salvi à Tripolis, entrée et per-
gola

Giovanni Pellegrini, 1933
Haus am Meer bei Tripolis
House by the sea near Tripoli
Maison au bord de la mer près de
Tripolis

Giovanni Pellegrini, 1934
Villa Salvi in Tripolis, Gesamtansicht
The Salvi villa in Tripoli. Overall
view
Villa Salvi à Tripolis, vue d'ensemble

M E X I K O

José Arnal
Bürogebäude in Mexiko, Straßen-
fassade
Office building in Mexico City.
Street facade
Bâtiment administratif à Mexico,
façade donnant sur la rue

**Enrique de la Mora y Palomar und
José Creixell M. 1935–1936**
Mietwohnhaus in Mexiko, Straßen-
fassade
Flats in Mexico City. Street facade
Immeuble à Mexico, façade don-
nant sur la rue

Juan O'Gorman
Atelier des Malers Diego Rivera in
San Angel, Mexiko, von der Straße
aus gesehen
Studio of the painter Diego Rivera
in San Angel, Mexico City. View
from the road
Atelier du peintre Diego Rivera à
San Angel, Mexico, vue de la rue

Juan O'Gorman
Atelier des Malers Cecil O'Gorman
in San Angel, Mexiko, vom Garten
aus gesehen
Studio of the painter Cecil O'Gorman in San Angel, Mexico City.
View from the garden
Atelier du peintre Cecil O'Gorman
à San Angel, Mexico, vu du jardin

**Enrique Yanez und Pedro Busta-
mente**
Mietwohnhaus in Mexiko
Flats in Mexico City
Immeuble à Mexico

NIEDERLANDE

Joh. W. E. Buys und J. B. Lürsen, 1928
Geschäftshaus »De Volharding« in Den Haag
The »De Volharding« store in The Hague
Immeuble commercial »De Volharding« à La Haye

**Johannes Andreas Brinkman und
L. C. van der Vlugt, 1933**
Haus Sonneveld in Rotterdam
The Sonneveld house in Rotterdam
Maison Sonneveld à Rotterdam

**Johannes Andreas Brinkman und
L. C. van der Vlugt, 1930**
Haus De Bruyn in Schiedam
The De Bruyn house in Schiedam
Maison De Bruyn à Schiedam

**Johannes Andreas Brinkman und
Johannes Hendrikus van den
Broek, 1935**
Seebahnhof der Holland-Amerika
Linie in Rotterdam, Wartesaal
Seaport of the Holland-American
Line. Waiting room
Gare maritime de la ligne Hol-
lande-Amérique à Rotterdam, salle
d'attente

**Johannes Andreas Brinkman und
L. C. van der Vlugt, 1927**
Tempel der Theosophen in Amster-
dam, Eingang
Theosophist temple in Amsterdam.
Entrance
Temple des théosophes à Amster-
dam, entrée

B. van Ravenstein, 1928
Wasserturm mit Büro- und Labor-
räumen in Roermond
Water tower with offices and
laboratories in Roermond
Château d'eau avec bureaux et
laboratoires à Roermond

**Johannes Andreas Brinkman und
L. C. van der Vlugt, 1931**
Geschäftshaus A. van Holker Zoonen in Rotterdam
The A. van Holker Zoonen store in Rotterdam
Immeuble commercial A. van Holker Zoonen à Rotterdam

**W. van Tijen, J. A. Brinkman und
L. C. van der Vlugt, 1934**
Wohnblock »Bergpolder« in Rotter-
dam, Ansicht von Südwesten
The »Bergpolder« block of flats in
Rotterdam. View from the south-
west
Bloc d'habitation »Bergpolder« à
Rotterdam, vue du sud-ouest

**W. van Tijen, J. A. Brinkman und
L. C. van der Vlugt, 1934**
Wohnblock »Bergpolder« in Rotter-
dam, Ansicht von Nordosten
The »Bergpolder« block of flats in
Rotterdam. View from the north-
east
Bloc d'habitation »Bergpolder« à
Rotterdam, vue du nord-est

**Johannes Andreas Brinkman und
L. C. van der Vlugt, 1930**
Fabrikgebäude der Tabakwarenfa-
brik van Nelle in Rotterdam
Van Nelle tobacco factory building
in Rotterdam
Bâtiment de l'usine de tabac Van
Nelle à Rotterdam

**Johannes Andreas Brinkman und
L. C. van der Vlugt, 1930**
Fabrikgebäude der Tabakwarenfabrik van Nelle in Rotterdam, ver-
glaster Übergang von den Büros
zur Fabrikation
Van Nelle tobacco factory building
in Rotterdam. Glazed passageway
between offices and production
area
Bâtiment de l'usine de tabac Van
Nelle à Rotterdam, passage vitré
des bureaux aux lieux de fabrication

**Johannes Andreas Brinkman und
L. C. van der Vlugt, 1930**
Tabakwarenfabrik van Nelle in
Rotterdam, Treppenhaus
Van Nelle tobacco factory building
in Rotterdam. Staircase
Bâtiment de l'usine de tabac Van
Nelle à Rotterdam, cage d'escalier

**Johannes Andreas Brinkman und
L. C. van der Vlugt, 1930**
Tabakwarenfabrik van Nelle in
Rotterdam, Cafeteria für das Perso-
nal im obersten Stock
Van Nelle tobacco factory building
in Rotterdam. Staff canteen on the
top floor
Bâtiment de l'usine de tabac Van
Nelle à Rotterdam, cafétéria pour
le personnel à l'étage supérieur

**Johannes Andreas Brinkman und
L. C. van der Vlugt**
Bankhaus R. Mees und Zoonen in
Rotterdam
R. Mees and Zoonen bank in Rotter-
dam
Immeuble de la banque R. Mees et
Zoonen à Rotterdam

Johannes Duiker, 1930
Freiluftschule in Amsterdam
Open-air school in Amsterdam
Ecole de plein air à Amsterdam

B. Bijvoet und J. Duiker, 1927
Sanatorium »Zonnenstraal« in Hilversum, Teilansicht
»Zonnenstraal« sanatorium in Hilversum. Partial view
Maison de santé »Zonnenstraal« à Hilversum, vue partielle

Johannes Bernardus van Loghem, 1933
Badeanstalt in Haarlem, Südseite mit Terrasse
Bathing establishment in Haarlem. South aspect with terrace
Etablissement de bains à Haarlem, côté sud avec terrasse

Johannes Bernardus van Loghem, 1933
Badeanstalt in Haarlem, die Schwimmhalle ist zur Terrasse geöffnet
Bathing establishment in Haarlem. The swimming pool is open to the terrace
Etablissement de bains à Haarlem, la halle de natation s'ouvre sur la terrasse

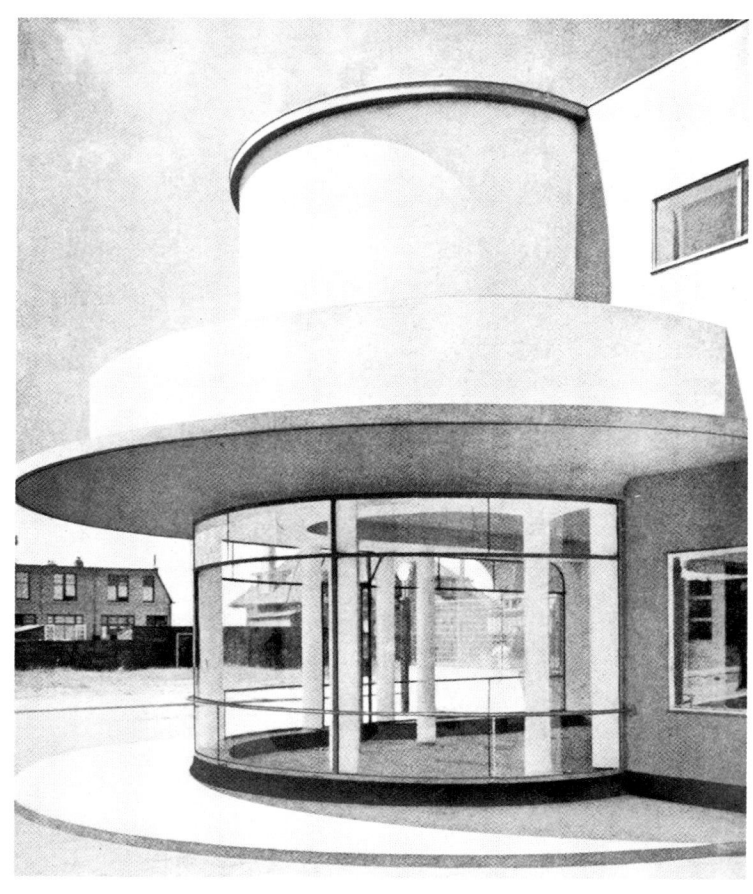

**Jacobus Johannes Pieter Oud,
1924–1927**
Kleinwohnungsanlage in Hoek van
Holland
Residential development in the
Hook of Holland
Complexe de petits appartements à
Hoek van Holland

**Jacobus Johannes Pieter Oud,
1924–1927**
Kleinwohnungsanlage in Hoek van
Holland, Ansicht des Kopfbaus
Residential development in the
Hook of Holland. View of end
block
Complexe de petits appartements à
Hoek van Holland, vue du bâtiment
de tête

**Jacobus Johannes Pieter Oud,
1925–1929**
Arbeitersiedlung »Kiefhoek« in
Rotterdam
»Kiefhoek« workers' estate in
Rotterdam
Lotissement d'ouvriers »Kiefhoek«
à Rotterdam

**Gerrit Rietveld und Truus Schröder-
Schräder, 1924**
Haus Schröder in Utrecht, Rückseite
The Schröder house in Utrecht. Rear
view
Maison Schröder à Utrecht, façade
postérieure

**Gerrit Rietveld und Truus Schröder-
Schräder, 1924**
Haus Schröder in Utrecht
The Schröder house in Utrecht
Maison Schröder à Utrecht

NORWEGEN

Aasland und Korsmo
Villa in Oslo
Villa in Oslo
Villa à Oslo

Nicolai Beer
Reihenhäuser in Oslo
Terrace houses in Oslo
Maison individuelle standard à
Oslo

**Gudolf Blakstad und Hermann
Munthe-Kaas**
Villa in Oslo, Straßenseite
Villa in Oslo. View from the road
Villa à Oslo, côté rue

ÖSTERREICH

Joseph F. Dex, 1932
Doppelhaus auf der Werkbundaus-
stellung in Wien, Straßenseite
Semi-detached houses at the Werk-
bund exhibition in Vienna. View
from the road
Maison double à l'exposition du
Werkbund à Vienne, côté rue

Joseph F. Dex, 1932
Doppelhaus auf der Werkbundaus-
stellung in Wien, Wohnraum und
Küche
Semi-detached houses at the Werk-
bund exhibition in Vienna.
Living room and kitchen
Maison double à l'exposition du
Werkbund à Vienne, salle de séjour
et cuisine

André Lurçat, 1932
Reihenhäuser auf der Werkbundausstellung in Wien, Gartenseite;
Straßenseite
Terrace houses at the Werkbund
exhibition in Vienna. View from the
garden. View from the road
Maisons individuelles standard à
l'exposition du Werkbund à Vienne,
côté jardin, côté rue

Gerrit Rietveld, 1932
Reihenhäuser auf der Werkbundausstellung in Wien, Gartenseite
Terrace houses at the Werkbund
exhibition in Vienna. View from the
garden
Maisons individuelles standard à
l'exposition du Werkbund à Vienne,
côté jardin

Oskar Strnad, 1932
Doppelhaus auf der Werkbundaus-
stellung in Wien
Semi-detached houses at the Werk-
bund exhibition in Vienna
Maison double à l'exposition du
Werkbund à Vienne

Ernst A. Plischke, 1932
Arbeitsamt in Liesing, Wien, Haupt-
fassade
Employment office in Liesing,
Vienna. Main facade
Agence pour l'emploi à Liesing,
Vienne, façade principale

Ernst A. Plischke, 1932
Arbeitsamt in Liesing, Wien, Treppenhaus
Employment office in Liesing, Vienna. Staircase
Agence pour l'emploi à Liesing, Vienne, cage d'escalier

Ernst A. Plischke, 1933–1934
Sommerhaus am Attersee, Vordach
an der Südseite
Summer-house at Attersee. Canopy
on the south side
Maison d'été au bord du lac Attersee, auvent côté sud

Ernst A. Plischke, 1933–1934
Sommerhaus am Attersee, Ansicht
vom See
Summer-house at Attersee. View
from the lake
Maison d'été au bord du lac Attersee, vue du lac

Ernst A. Plischke, 1933–1934
Sommerhaus am Attersee, Terrasse
Summer-house at Attersee. Terrace
Maison d'été au bord du lac Atter-
see, terrasse

Otto Ernst Schweizer, 1929—1931
Stadion in Wien, Außenansicht
Stadium in Vienna. Exterior view
Stade à Vienne, vue de l'extérieur

Otto Ernst Schweizer, 1929—1931
Stadion in Wien, Tribüne
Stadium in Vienna. Grandstand
Stade à Vienne, tribunes

Otto Ernst Schweizer, 1929–1931
Stadion in Wien, Zugang zur Tri-
büne
Stadium in Vienna. Entrance to the
grandstand
Stade à Vienne, accès aux tribunes

Lois Welzenbacher
Pension »Turm« in Hall, Tirol, Süd-
seite
Pension »Turm« in Hall, Tyrol.
South view
Pension »Turm« à Hall, Tyrol, côté
sud

Lois Welzenbacher
Pension »Turm« in Hall, Tirol, West-seite
Pension »Turm« in Hall, Tyrol. West view
Pension »Turm« à Hall, Tyrol, côté ouest

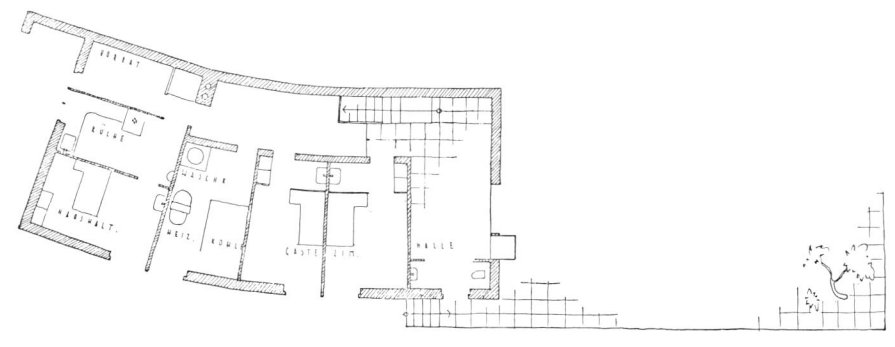

Lois Welzenbacher
Villa in Zell am See, Gesamtansicht; Grundriß
Villa in Zell am See. Overall view; ground plan
Villa à Zell am See, vue d'ensemble; plan

Lois Welzenbacher, 1929
Wohnhaus »Treichl« in Innsbruck,
Südfassade
»Treichl« residence in Innsbruck,
South facade
Immeuble »Treichl« à Innsbruck,
façade sud

P O L E N

Hans Scharoun, 1929
Wohnheim auf der Werkbundaus-
stellung in Breslau, Terrassenseite
Hostel building at the Werkbund
exhibition in Breslau. Terrace side
Foyer d'habitation à l'exposition du
Werkbund à Breslau, côté terrasse

Hans Scharoun, 1929
Wohnheim auf der Werkbundausstellung in Breslau, Flügel mit Zwei-
bettzimmern
Hostel building at the Werkbund
exhibition in Breslau. Double bedroom wing
Foyer d'habitation à l'exposition du
Werkbund à Breslau, aile avec
chambres à deux lits

Adolf Rading, 1929
Wohnhaus auf der Werkbundausstellung in Breslau, Westfassade
(oben); Ostfassade (unten)
House at the Werkbund exhibition
in Breslau. West facade (above).
East facade (below)
Immeuble à l'exposition du Werkbund à Breslau, façade ouest (en
haut); façade est (en bas)

Moritz Hadda, 1929
Einfamilienhaus auf der Werkbundausstellung in Breslau
Detached house at the Werkbund
exhibition in Breslau
Maison d'habitation individuelle à
l'exposition du Werkbund à Breslau

Heinrich Lauterbach, 1929
Einfamilienhaus auf der Werkbundausstellung in Breslau, im Hintergrund das Haus von Moritz Hadda
Detached house at the Werkbund
exhibition in Breslau. In the background, the house by Moritz Hadda
Maison d'habitation individuelle à
l'exposition du Werkbund à Breslau, au fond la maison de Moritz
Hadda

Jósef Szanajca, 1933
Wohnsiedlung »Z.U.P. U.« in War-
schau, Hofseite
»Z.U.P. U.« housing estate in
Warsaw. View from the courtyard
Lotissement d'habitation
»Z.U.P. U.« à Varsovie, côté cour

Barbara und Stanislaw Brukalski
Genossenschaftliche Wohnsiedlung in Warschau, Bauteil IV, Straßenansicht
Cooperative housing estate in Warsaw. Section IV. View from the road
Lotissement d'habitation coopératif
à Varsovie, bâtiment IV, vue de la
rue

Bohdan Lachert und Jósef Szanajca, 1928
Dreifamilienhaus in Warschau, Südseite
House for three families in Warsaw. South view
Maison d'habitation pour trois ménages à Varsovie, côté sud

**Bohdan Lachert und Jósef
Szanajca, 1928**
Dreifamilienhaus in Warschau,
Gartenseite (oben); Straßenseite
(unten)
House for three families in Warsaw.
View from the garden (above).
View from the road (below)
Maison d'habitation pour trois
ménages à Varsovie, côté jardin
(en haut); côte rue (en bas)

Helena und Szymon Syrkus mit Stanislaw Hempel, 1932
Haus Dr. N. in Warschau, Südseite
House of Dr. N. in Warsaw. South side
Maison du Dr N. à Varsovie, côté sud

**Helena und Szymon Syrkus mit
Stanislaw Hempel, 1932**
Haus Dr. N. in Warschau, Ostseite;
Grundrisse von Erdgeschoß und
erstem Stock
House of Dr. N. in Warsaw. East
side; ground-floor and first-floor
plans
Maison du Dr N. à Varsovie, côté
est; plans du rez-de-chaussée et du
premier étage

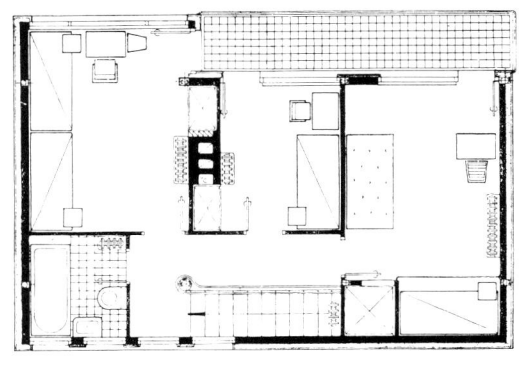

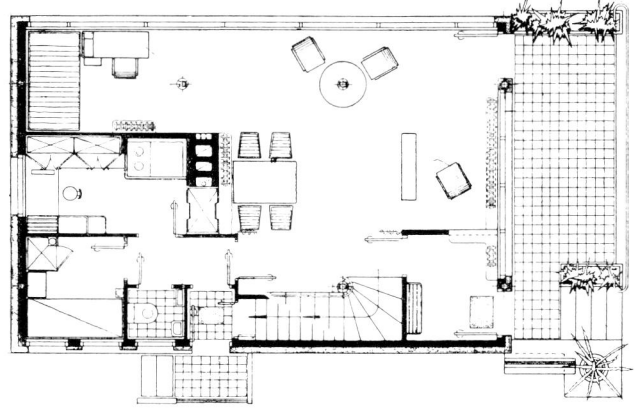

RUMÄNIEN

Marcel und Juliu Iancu, 1937
Haus Reich in Bukarest, Straßenseite
The Reich house in Bucharest. View
from the road
Maison Reich à Bucarest, côté donnant sur la rue

Marcel und Juliu Iancu, 1936
Sanatorium »Bucegi« in Predeal,
von Westen gesehen
»Bucegi« sanatorium in Predeal.
View from the west
Maison de santé »Bucegi« à Pre-
deal, vue de l'ouest

Marcel und Juliu Iancu, 1936
Sanatorium »Bucegi« in Predeal,
von Osten gesehen
»Bucegi« sanatorium in Predeal.
View from the east
Maison de santé »Bucegi« à Pre-
deal, vue de l'est

S C H W E D E N

Erik Gunnar Asplund, 1930
Restaurant auf der Stockholmer
Ausstellung, Balkon vor dem Tanz-
saal (oben); Caféterrasse (unten)
Restaurant at the Stockholm Exhibition. Balcony in front of the ball-
room (above). Cafe terrace (below)
Restaurant à l'exposition de Stockholm, balcon devant la salle de
danse (en haut); terrasse du café
(en bas)

Paul Hedqvist
Stadion in Kristineberg, Eingangs-seite
Stadium in Kristineberg. Entrance side
Stade à Kristineberg, côté de l'entrée

Paul Hedqvist
Schwimmbad in Eskilstuna, Sprung-
turm
Swimming pool in Eskilstuna.
Diving-board tower
Piscine à Eskilstuna, plongeoir

Paul Hedqvist
Stadion in Kristineberg, Tribünen-
bau
Swimming pool in Kristinenberg,
Grandstand
Stade à Kristineberg, bâtiment des
tribunes

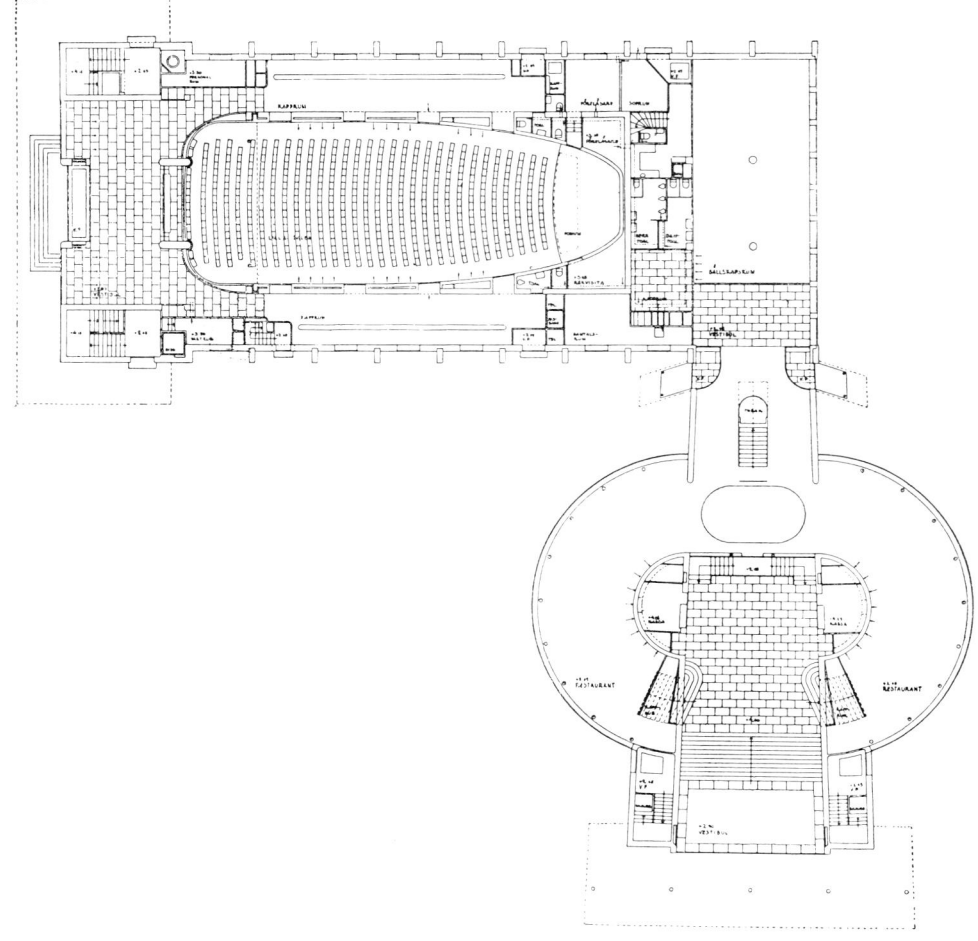

Sven Markelius, 1934
Konzerthalle in Helsingborg, Ein-
gangsseite; Grundriß
Concert hall in Helsingborg.
Entrance side; ground plan
Halle des concerts à Helsingborg,
côté de l'entrée; plan

Sven Markelius, 1934
Konzerthalle in Helsingborg, Vestibül (oben); Eingang bei Nacht (unten)
Concert hall in Helsingborg. Foyer (above). Entrance at night (below)
Halle des concerts à Helsingborg, hall d'entrée (en haut); entrée de nuit (en bas)

**Sven Markelius und Uno Ahren,
1931**
Studentenhaus der Technischen
Hochschule in Stockholm, Ansicht
und Grundriß
Students' residence at the Institute
of Science and Technology in
Stockholm. View and ground plan
Maison d'étudiants de l'Université
Technique de Stockholm, vue de
face et plan

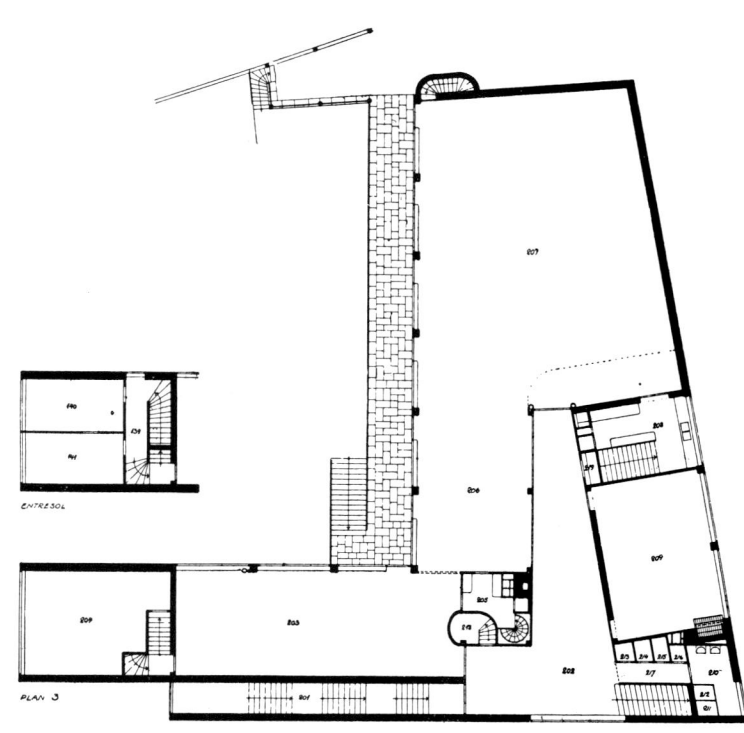

Sven Markelius
Hangar des Flughafens in Stockholm
Hangar at Stockholm airport
Hangar de l'aéroport à Stockholm

**Bauabteilung der Konsumgenos-
senschaft Stockholm**
Fabrikgebäude der Konsumgenos-
senschaft in Stockholm, Gesamtansicht
Factory building of the Consumer
Cooperative in Stockholm. Overall
view
Bâtiment d'usine de la Coopérative
des Consommateurs à Stockholm,
vue d'ensemble

SCHWEIZ

Werner M. Moser
Doppelhaus in Zürich, Südseite
Semi-detached houses in Zurich.
South view
Maison double à Zurich, côté sud

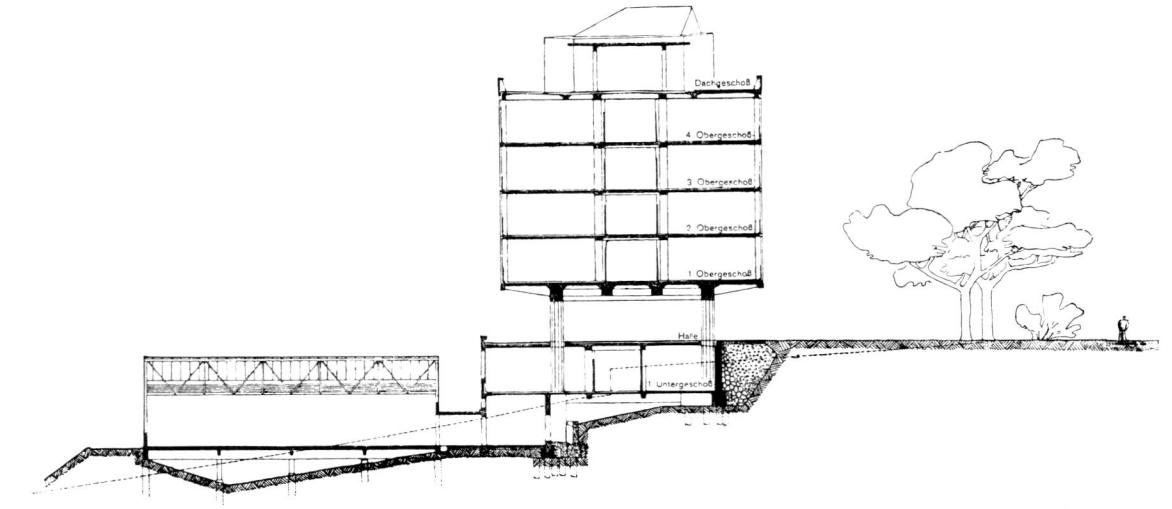

Hans Brechbühler, 1935
Landwirtschaftliches Lagerge-
bäude in Köniz, Bern
Agricultural storage building in
Köniz, Bern
Bâtiment de stockage agricole à
Köniz, Berne

Hans Brechbühler, 1937–1939
Schule für Kunst und Handwerk in
Bern, Schnitt
School of Art and Crafts in Bern.
Section
Ecole des Beaux-Arts et de l'Artisa-
nat à Berne, coupe

Hans Brechbühler, 1937–1939
Schule für Kunst und Handwerk in
Bern, Ansicht von der Straße
School of Art and Crafts in Bern.
View from the road
Ecole des Beaux-Arts et de l'Artisa-
nat à Berne, vue de la rue

Hans Brechbühler, 1937–1939
Schule für Kunst und Handwerk in
Bern, Rückseite mit vorgelagertem
Werkstättengebäude
School of Art and Crafts in Bern.
Rear view showing separate work-
shop building
Ecole des Beaux-Arts et de l'Artisa-
nat à Berne, côté postérieur avec
bâtiments des ateliers formant sail-
lie

**Karl Egender und Ernst F.
Burckhardt**
Johanneskirche in Basel, Gesamt-
ansicht; Innenansicht
Johanneskirche in Basle. Overall
view. Interior view
Eglise St Jean à Bâle, vue d'ensem-
ble; rue de l'intérieur

Karl Egender und Ernst F. Burckhardt
Johanneskirche in Basel, Glocken-turm
Johanneskirche in Basle. Bell-tower
Eglise St Jean à Bâle, clocher

**Le Corbusier und Pierre Jeanneret,
1932**
Wohnhaus »Clarté« in Genf, Teil
der Hauptfassade
The »Clarté« house in Geneva. Part
of main facade
Immeuble »Clarté« à Genève, partie de la façade principale

Le Corbusier und Pierre Jeanneret, 1932
Wohnhaus »Clarté« in Genf, Treppenhaus
The »Clarté« house in Geneva. Staircase
Immeuble »Clarté« à Genève, cage d'escalier

Francis Quétant, 1935
Wohnblock in Genf
Residential block in Geneva
Bloc d'habitation à Genève

Francis Quétant
Villa Meyer in Cologny, Genf, Stra-
ßenseite
The Meyer Villa in Cologne,
Geneva. View from the road
Villa Meyer à Cologny, Genève,
côté rue

Henri Robert von der Mühll, 1933
Wohnhaus »La Chandoline« in
Lausanne, Gartenseite
The house »La Chandoline« in
Lausanne. View from the garden
Immeuble »La Chandoline« à Lau-
sanne, côté jardin

Alfred und Emil Roth mit Marcel Breuer, 1935–1936
Wohnhäuser in Doldertal, Zürich, Südseite
Houses in Doldertal, Zurich. South view
Maisons d'habitation à Doldertal, Zurich, côté sud

Alfred und Emil Roth mit Marcel Breuer, 1935–1936
Wohnhäuser in Doldertal, Zürich, Ostseite eines Gebäudes
Houses in Doldertal, Zurich. One of the buildings viewed from the east
Maisons d'habitation à Doldertal, Zurich, côté ouest d'un bâtiment

Alfred und Emil Roth mit Marcel Breuer, 1935–1936
Wohnhäuser in Doldertal, Zürich, Gesamtansicht
Houses in Doldertal, Zurich. Overall view
Maisons d'habitation à Doldertal, Zurich, vue d'ensemble

Alfred Roth
Fabrikgebäude in Wangen, Ostseite
Factory building in Wangen. View
from the east
Bâtiments d'usine à Wangen, côté
est

Alfred Roth
Fabrikgebäude in Wangen, Nordseite
Factory building in Wangen. View
from the north
Bâtiments d'usine à Wangen, côté
nord

Alberto Sartoris, 1934–1935
Haus des Weinbauern Morand-
Pasteur in Saillon, Vallese, Ansich-
ten; Grundrisse
House of the vintner Morand-Pas-
teur in Saillon, Vallese. Views. Plans
Maison du vigneron Morand-Pas-
teur à Saillon, Vallese, vues; plans

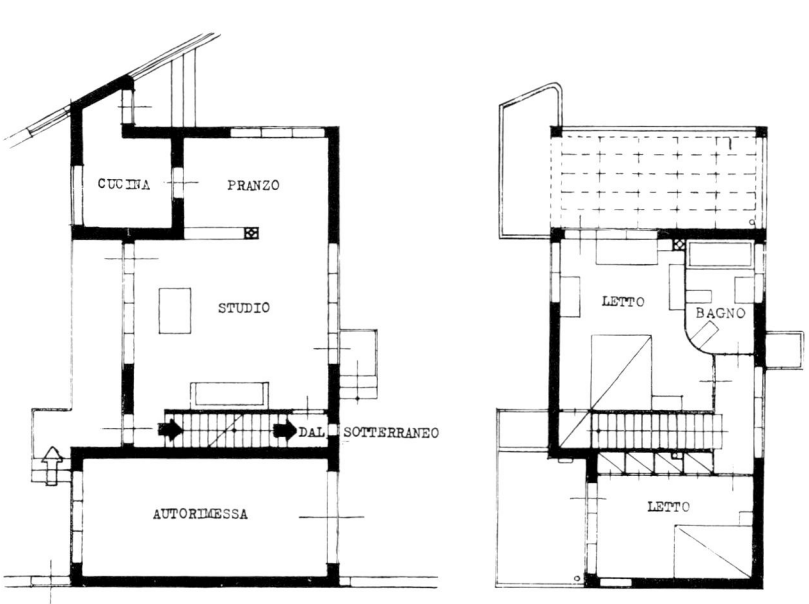

Alberto Sartoris, 1938–1939
Atelierhaus der Maler Italo und
Vincenzo de Grando in Corseaux-
Vevey, Vaud, Südseite mit Aus-
sichtsbalkon
Studio house of the painters Italo
and Vincenzo de Grando in
Corseaux-Vevey, Vaud, South side
with panoramic balcony
Maison atelier des peintres Italo et
Vincenzo de Grando à Corseaux-
Vevey, Vaud, côté sud avec balcon
panoramique

Alberto Sartoris, 1938–1939
Atelierhaus der Maler Italo und
Vincenzo de Grando in Corseaux-
Vevey, Vaud, Ansicht von Südosten
Studio house of the painters Italo
and Vincenzo de Grando in
Corseaux-Vevey, Vaud. View from
the south-east
Maison atelier des peintres Italo et
Vincenzo de Grando à Corseaux-
Vevey, Vaud, vue côté sud-est

Alberto Sartoris, 1938–1939
Atelierhaus der Maler Italo und
Vincenzo de Grando in Corseaux-
Vevey, Vaud, Nordseite mit großem
Atelierfenster
Studio house of the painters Italo
and Vincenzo de Grando in
Corseaux-Vevey, Vaud. North side
with large studio window
Maison atelier des peintres Italo et
Vincenzo de Grando à Corseaux-
Vevey, Vaud, côté nord avec
grande fenêtre d'atelier

Hans Schmidt und Paul Artaria
Villa in Basel, Längs- und Seitenansicht
Villa in Basle, Longitudinal and side view
Villa à Bâle, vue longitudinale et latérale

Otto und Walter Senn, 1935
Villa in Gerzensee, Bern, Ansicht
von Süden und Norden
Villa in Gerzensee, Bern. View from
the north and the south
Villa à Gerzensee, Berne, vue du
sud et du nord

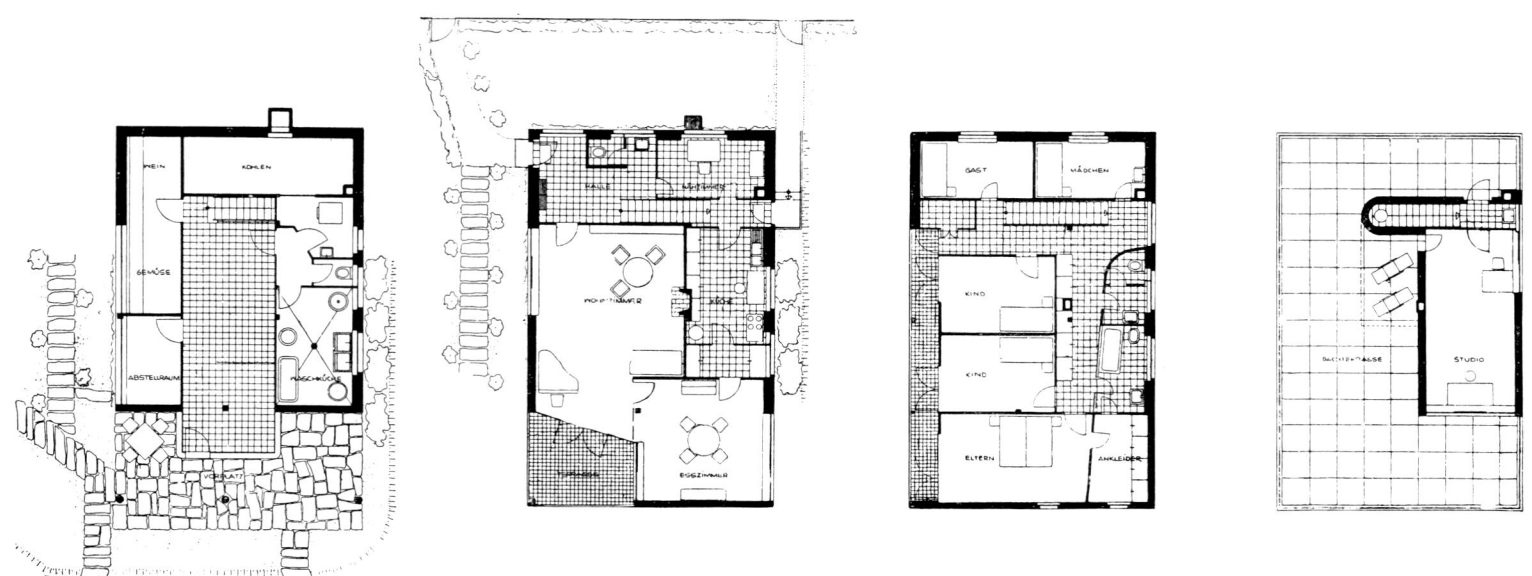

Otto Senn, 1936
Villa in Binningen, Basel, vom Garten her gesehen
Villa in Binningen, Basle. View from
the garden
Villa à Binningen, Bâle, vue du jardin

Otto Senn, 1936
Villa in Binningen, Basel, von der
Straße aus gesehen; Grundrisse
Villa in Binningen, Basle. View from
the road; plans
Villa à Binningen, Bâle, vue de la
rue; plans

Rudolf Steiger und Hubacher
Haus »Zett« in Zürich, Innenansicht
des »Roxy«-Kinos mit geöffnetem
Dach
»Zett« building in Zurich. Interior
view of the Roxy Cinema with roof
open
Maison »Zett« à Zurich, vue de l'intérieur du cinéma »Roxy« avec toit
ouvert

Rudolf Steiger und Hubacher
Haus »Zett« in Zürich, Rückansicht
mit dem Schiebedach des Kinos
»Zett« building in Zurich. Rear view
showing the cinema's sliding roof
Maison »Zett« à Zurich, vue postérieure avec le toit coulissant du
cinéma

Rudolf Steiger und Hubacher
Haus »Zett« in Zürich, Straßenfassade
»Zett« building in Zurich. Street facade
Maison »Zett« à Zurich, façade donnant sur la rue

SOWJETUNION

Boris M. Welikowski, 1925–1927
Gebäude des »Gostorg« in
Moskau, Treppenhaus
»Gostorg« building in Moscow.
Staircase
Bâtiment du »Gostorg« à Moscou,
cage d'escalier

Boris M. Welikowski, 1925–1927
Gebäude des »Gostorg« in
Moskau, Straßenansicht
»Gostorg« building in Moscow.
Street facade
Bâtiment du »Gostorg« à Moscou,
façade donnant sur la rue

Moissej J. Ginsburg, 1932
Volkshaus in Moskau, Gartenseite
House of the People in Moscow.
View from the garden
Maison populaire à Moscou, côté
jardin

Moissej J. Ginsburg
Wohnhaus in Moskau
Flats in Moscow
Immeuble à Moscou

Alexander Nürnberg, 1938
Hotel »Vasa« in Pärnu
Hotel »Vasa« in Pärnu
Hôtel »Vasa« à Pärnu

Alexej W. Stschussew
Erholungsheim in Macest, Ansicht
vom Garten; Dachterrasse
Convalescent home in Macest.
View from the garden; roof terrace
Maison de repos à Macest, vue du
jardin; terrasse sur le toit

**Alexander W. Kusnezow mit W. und
G. Mowtschan, A. Fissenko,
I. Nikolajew, L. Meilman,
G. Karlsen, 1927–1929**
Allunionsinstitut für Elektrotechnik
in Moskau, Laboratorium für
Apparatebau
All-Union Institute of Electrical
Engineering in Moscow. Laboratory
for machine engineering
Institut Allunion d'électrotechnique
à Moscou, laboratoire de construc-
tion d'appareils

**Alexander W. Kusnezow mit W. und
G. Mowtschan, A. Fissenko,
I. Nikolajew, L. Meilman,
G. Karlsen, 1927–1929**
Allunionsinstitut für Elektrotechnik
in Moskau, Hochspannungslabora-
torium
All-union Institute of Electrical
Engineering in Moscow. High-vol-
tage laboratory
Institut Allunion d'électrotechnique
à Moscou, laboratoire de haute
tension

**Alexander W. Kusnezow mit W. und
G. Mowtschan, A. Fissenko,
I. Nikolajew, L. Meilman,
G. Karlsen, 1927–1929**
Allunionsinstitut für Elektrotechnik
in Moskau, Elektrophysikalisches
Laboratorium
All-union Institute of Electrical
Engineering in Moscow.
Electrophysics laboratory
Institut Allunion d'électrotechnique
à Moscou, laboratoire électro-phy-
sique

**Alexander W. Kusnezow mit
A. Fissenko und I. Nikolajew, 1928**
Inst tut der Textilindustrie in
Moskau, Laboratorium für Wolle
Textile Industry Institute in Moscow,
Wool laboratory
Inst tut de l'industrie textile à Mos-
cou, laboratoire d'étude de la laine

SPANIEN

Sixto Illescas
Haus »Vilaró« in Sant Josep de la
Montanya, Barcelona, Balkon
The »Vilaro« house in Sant Josep
de la Montanya, Barcelona. Bal-
cony
Maison »Villaró« à Sant Josep de
la Montanya, Barcelone, balcon

**Architekten der G.A.T.E.P.A.C.,
1935**
Wohnsiedlung in Barcelona
Housing estate in Barcelona
Lotissement à Barcelone

Sixto Illescas
Haus »Vilaró« in Sant Josep de la
Montanya, Barcelona, Teilansicht
der Fassade
The »Vilaro« house in Sant Josep
de la Montanya, Barcelona. Partial
view of the facade
Maison »Villaró« à Sant Josep de
la Montanya, Barcelone, vue partielle de la façade

Ludwig Mies van der Rohe, 1929
Deutscher Pavillon auf der Internationalen Ausstellung in Barcelona, Eingang
German pavilion at the International Exhibition in Barcelona. Entrance
Pavillon allemand à l'Exposition Internationale à Barcelone, entrée

Ludwig Mies van der Rohe, 1929
Deutscher Pavillon auf der Internationalen Ausstellung in Barcelona, Blick über das Wasserbecken
German pavilion at the International Exhibition in Barcelona. View of the pond
Pavillon allemand à l'Exposition Internationale à Barcelone, vue sur le bassin

Ludwig Mies van der Rohe, 1929
Deutscher Pavillon auf der Internationalen Ausstellung in Barcelona, Innenansicht
German pavilion at the International Exhibition in Barcelona. Interior view
Pavillon allemand à l'Exposition Internationale à Barcelone, vue intérieure

Fernando Garcia Mercadal
Wohnhaus in Madrid, Dachgarten
Flats in Madrid. Roof garden
Immeuble à Madrid, jardin sur le
toit

R. Duran Reinals, 1935
Mietwohnhaus »Aribau« in
Barcelona
»Aribau« flats in Barcelona
Immeuble »Aribau« à Barcelone

José Luis Sert, 1930
Mietwohnhaus »Muntaner« in
Barcelona, Straßenansicht; jede
Wohnung erstreckt sich über zwei
Stockwerke
»Muntaner« flats in Barcelona.
View from the road: each flat is on
two storeys
Immeuble »Muntaner« à Barcelone,
façade donnant sur la rue, chaque
appartement s'étend sur deux
étages

José Luis Sert
Juweliergeschäft »Roca« in
Barcelona
»Roca« jewelry shop in Barcelona
Bijouterie »Roca« à Barcelone

José Luis Sert, 1930
Mietwohnhaus »Muntaner« in
Barcelona
»Muntaner« flats in Barcelona
Immeuble »Muntaner« à Barcelone,
vue latérale

José Luis Sert, 1930
Mietwohnhaus »Muntaner« in
Barcelona, Treppenhaus
»Muntaner« flats in Barcelona.
Staircase
Immeuble »Muntaner« à Barcelone,
cage d'escalier

SÜDAFRIKA

Hanson, Tomkin und Finkelstein, 1933
Landhaus von Arthur Harris in Lower Houghton, Johannesburg
Country house of Arthur Harris in Lower Houghton, Johannesburg.
Maison de campagne d'Arthur Harris à Lower Houghton, Johannesburg

TSCHECHOSLOWAKEI

Alois Balán und Jiři Grossmann, 1929
Villa K. Jarone in Preßburg
Villa of K. Jarone in Bratislava
Villa K. Jarone à Bratislava

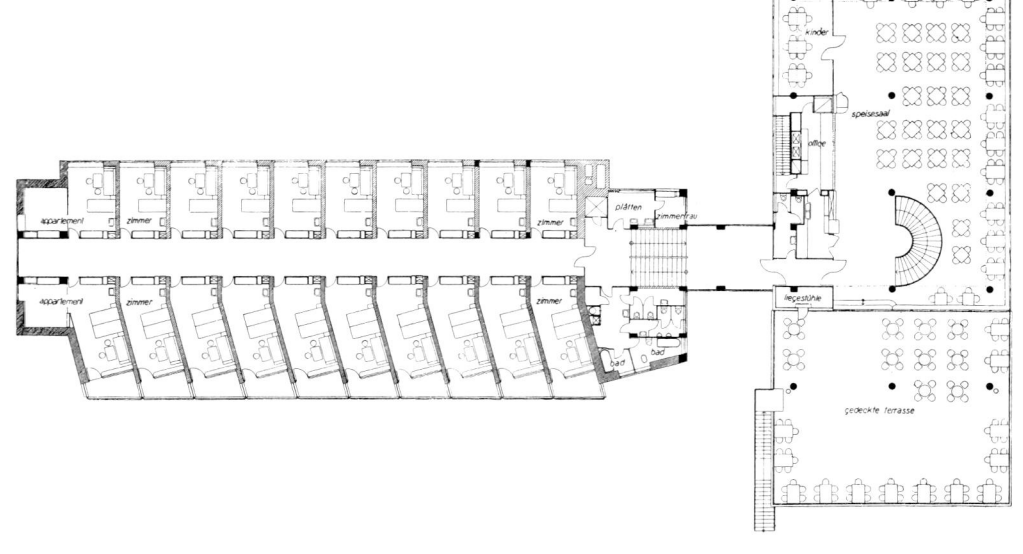

Bohuslav Fuchs und Karl Ernstberger
Erholungsheim »Morava« in Tatranská Lomnica, Ansicht des Bettentrakts; Grundriß
»Morava« convalescent home in Tatranská Lomnica. View of the bedroom wing; ground plan
Maison de repos »Morava« à Tatranská Lomnica, vue de l'aile où sont placés les lits; plan

Bohuslav Fuchs und Karl Ernstberger
Erholungsheim »Morava« in Tatranská Lomnica, Gesamtansicht; Blick auf die Terrassenanlage
»Morava« convalescence home in Tatranská Lomnica. Overall view. View of the terrace
Maison de repos »Morava« à Tatranská Lomnica, vue d'ensemble; vue sur le complexe de terrasses

**Bohuslav Fuchs und Josef Polášek,
1929–1930**
Mädchenberufsschule in Brünn,
Ansicht der Turnhalle und der
Unterrichtsräume
Girls' Vocational School in Brno.
View of the gymnasium and the
classrooms
Ecole professionnelle de filles à
Brno, vue du gymnase et des salles
de cours

**Bohuslav Fuchs und Josef Polášek,
1929–1930**
Mädchenberufsschule in Brünn,
Ansicht von der Straße
Girls' Vocational School in Brno.
View from the road
Ecole professionnelle de filles à
Brno, vue de la rue

**Bohuslav Fuchs und Josef Polášek,
1929–1930**
Mädchenberufsschule in Brünn,
Ansicht des Treppenhauses mit
Außengängen
Girls' Vocational School in Brno.
View of the staircase with exterior
passageways
Ecole professionnelle de filles à
Brno, vue de la cage d'escalier
avec couloirs extérieurs

**Bohuslav Fuchs und Josef Polášek,
1929–1930**
Mädchenberufsschule in Brünn,
Turnhalle
Girl's Vocational School in Brno.
Gymnasium
Ecole professionnelle de filles à
Brno, gymnase

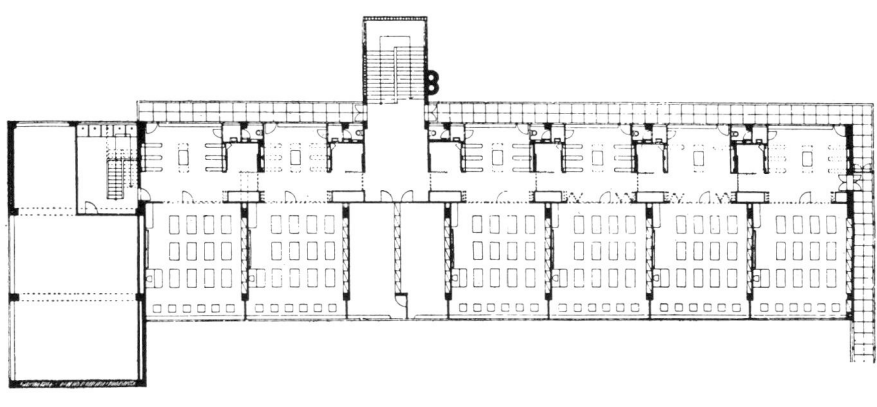

**Bohuslav Fuchs und Josef Polášek,
1929–1930**
Mädchenberufsschule in Brünn,
Durchgang zum Wohnheim;
Grundriß
Girls' Vocational School in Brno.
Passageway to hall of residence.
Ground plan
Ecole professionnelle de filles à
Brno, passage vers le foyer; plan

Josef Fuchs und Oldřich Tyl, 1925
Gebäude der Mustermesse in Prag
Trade fair building in Prague
Bâtiments de la foire des modèles à
Prague

Josef Gočár
Schule in Königgrätz, Heizanlage
mit Kindergarten
School in Königgrätz. Heating plant
and kindergarten building
Ecole à Königgrätz, installation de
chauffage et jardin d'enfants

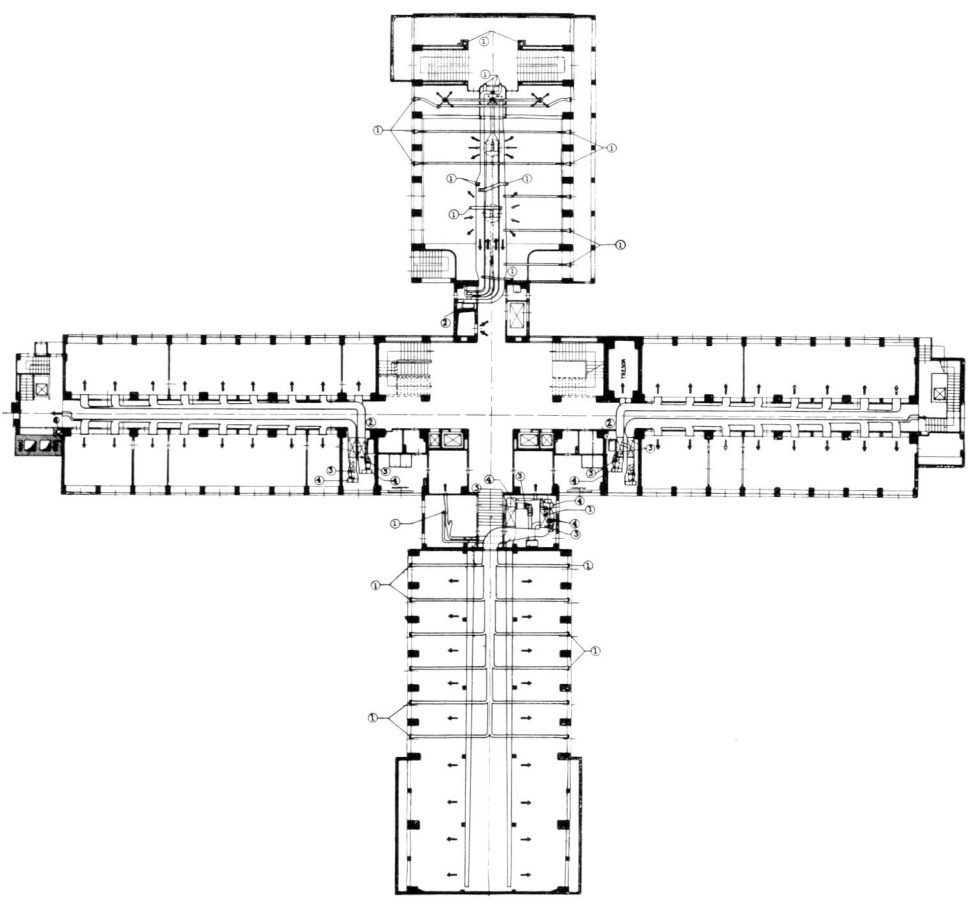

**Josef Havlíček und Karel Honzík,
1932—1933**
Sitz der Pensionskasse in Prag,
Westseite; Grundriß mit Lüftungs-
anlage
Headquarters of pension bank in
Prague. West view; ground plan
with ventilation plant
Siège de la caisse des pensions à
Prague, côté ouest; plan avec ins-
tallation d'aération

**Josef Havlíček und Karel Honzík,
1932–1933**
Sitz der Pensionskasse in Prag,
Ostseite
Headquarters of pension bank in
Prague. East view
Siège de la caisse des pensions à
Prague, côté est

**Josef Havlíček und Karel Honzík,
1932–1933**
Sitz der Pensionskasse in Prag,
Garagenhof
Headquarters of pension bank in
Prague. Garage area
Siège de la caisse des pensions à
Prague, cour de garage

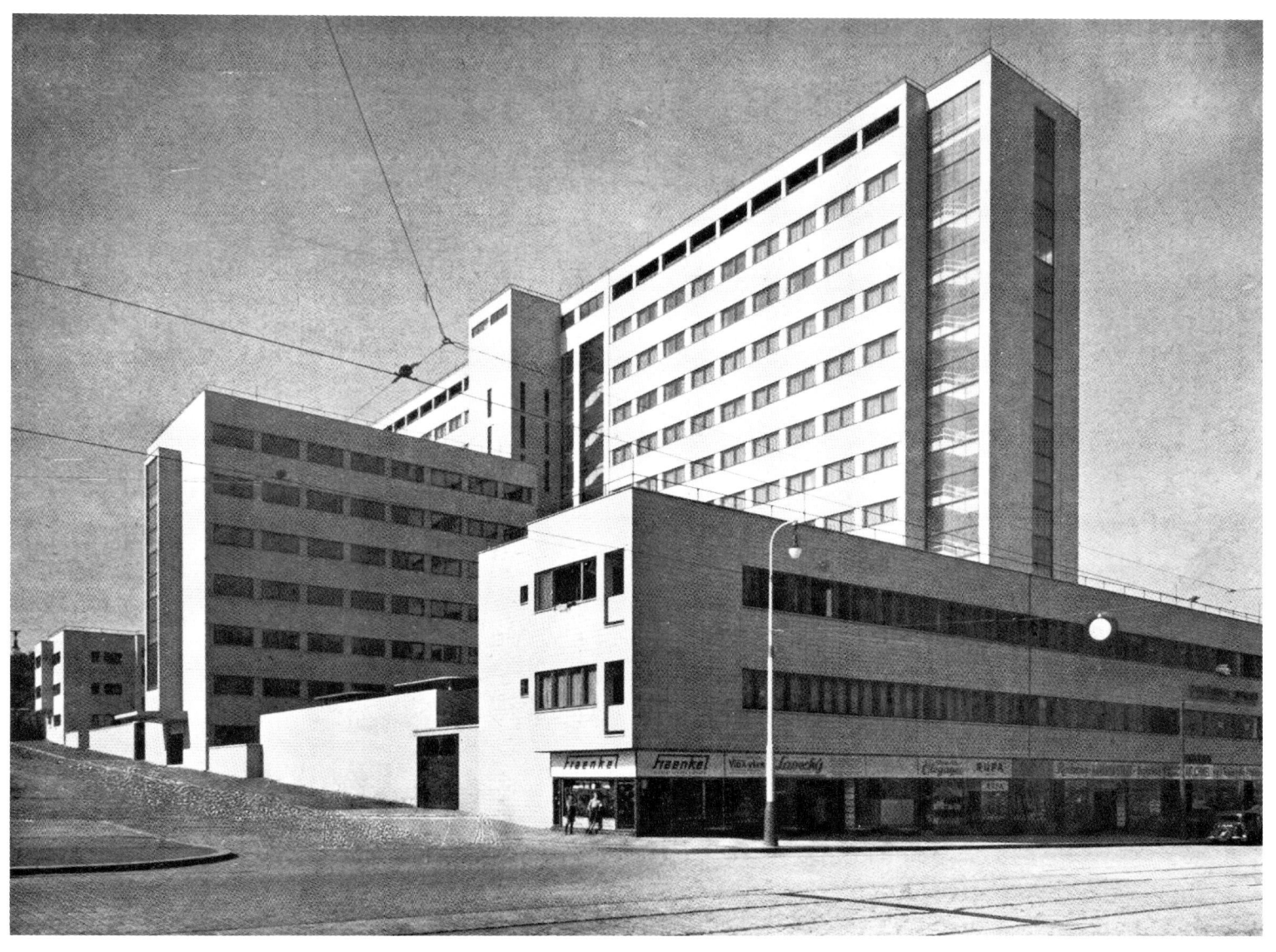

**Josef Havlíček und Karel Honzík,
1932–1933**
Sitz der Pensionskasse in Prag,
Ansicht von Nordosten
Headquarters of pension bank in
Prague. View from the north-east
Siège de la caisse des pensions à
Prague, vue du nord-est

Lud. Kyselka, 1928
Geschäftshaus »U Styblu« in Preß-
burg
»U Styblu« store in Bratislava
Immeuble commercial »U Styblu« à
Bratislava

Jaromir Krejcar
Geschäftshaus »Olympic« in Prag
»Olympic« store in Prague
Immeuble commercial »Olympic« à
Prague

Mojmir Kyselka, 1930
Volksschule in Brünn, Straßenfassade
Elementary school in Brno. Street
facade
Ecole primaire à Brno, façade donnant sur la rue

Mojmir Kyselka, 1930
Volksschule in Brünn, Eingang
Elementary school in Brno.
Entrance
Ecole primaire à Brno, entrée

Josef Havlíček und Karel Honzík
Landhaus in Prag
Country house in Prague
Maison de campagne à Prague

Heinrich Lauterbach
Haus Hasek in Gablonz, Ansicht
von Westen
The Hasek house in Gablonz. View
from the west
Maison Hasek à Gablonz, vue de
l'ouest

Heinrich Lauterbach
Haus Hasek in Gablonz, Ansicht
von Nordwesten
The Hasek house in Gablonz. View
from the north-west
Maison Hasek à Gablonz, vue du
nord-ouest

Heinrich Lauterbach
Haus Hasek in Gablonz, Terrasse,
von Süden gesehen
The Hasek house in Gablonz. South
view of terrace
Maison Hasek à Gablonz, terrasse
vue du sud

Heinrich Lauterbach
Haus Hasek in Gablonz, Treppen-
aufgang
The Hasek house in Gablonz. Stairs
Maison Hasek à Gablonz, montée
d'escalier

Ludwig Mies van der Rohe, 1931
Haus Tugendhat in Brünn, Eingang;
Straßenseite
The Tugendhat house in Brno.
Entrance. View from the road
Maison Tugendhat à Brno, entrée;
côté rue

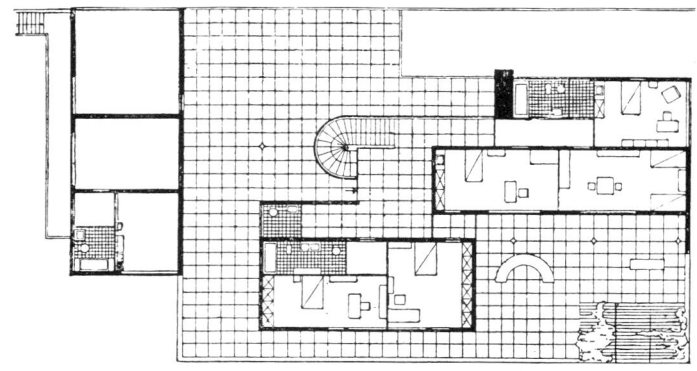

Ludwig Mies van der Rohe, 1931
Haus Tugendhat in Brünn, Gartenseite; Grundriß des ersten Stocks
The Tugendhat house in Brno. View
from the garden; first-floor plan
Maison Tugendhat à Brno, côté jardin; plan du premier étage

Ludwig Mies van der Rohe, 1931
Haus Tugendhat in Brünn, Gartenseite; Grundriß des Erdgeschosses
The Tugendhat house in Brno. View
from the garden. Plan of the ground
floor
Maison Tugendhat à Brno, côté jardin; plan du rez-de-chaussée

Ludwig Mies van der Rohe, 1931
Haus Tugendhat in Brünn, Wohn-
und Arbeitsbereich sind durch eine
Wand aus Onyx getrennt
The Tugendhat house in Brno. Living and work areas are separated
by an onyx wall
Maison Tugendhat à Brno, une
paroi d'onyx sépare les zones d'habitation et de travail

Ludwig Mies van der Rohe, 1931
Haus Tugendhat in Brünn, eine
halbrunde Ebenholzwand
umschließt den Eßtisch
The Tugendhat house in Brno. A
semi-circular ebony wall surrounds
the dining table
Maison Tugendhat à Brno, une
paroi de bois d'ébène semi-circu-
laire entoure la table à manger

Ludwig Mies van der Rohe, 1931
Haus Tugendhat in Brünn, Fenster-
front vor Eß- und Wohnbereich
The Tugendhat house in Brno. Window frontage of the dining and living area
Maison Tugendhat à Brno, ensemble de fenêtres devant les salles à
manger et de séjour

E. Mühlstein und V. Fürth
Haus Schück in Prag, Terrasse
The Schück house in Prague. Ter-
race
Maison Schück à Prague, terrasse

E. Mühlstein und V. Fürth
Haus Schück in Prag, Ansicht von
der Zufahrt
The Schück house in Prague. View
of the driveway
Maison Schück à Prague, vue de la
voie d'accès

UNGARN

József Fischer, 1934
Villa Hoffmann in Budapest,
Ansicht von Nordosten
The Hoffmann Villa in Budapest.
View from the north-east
Villa Hoffmann à Budapest, vue du
nord-est

József Fischer, 1934
Villa Hoffmann in Budapest,
Ansicht von Nordwesten
The Hoffmann Villa in Budapest.
View from the north-west
Villa Hoffmann à Budapest, vue du
nord-ouest

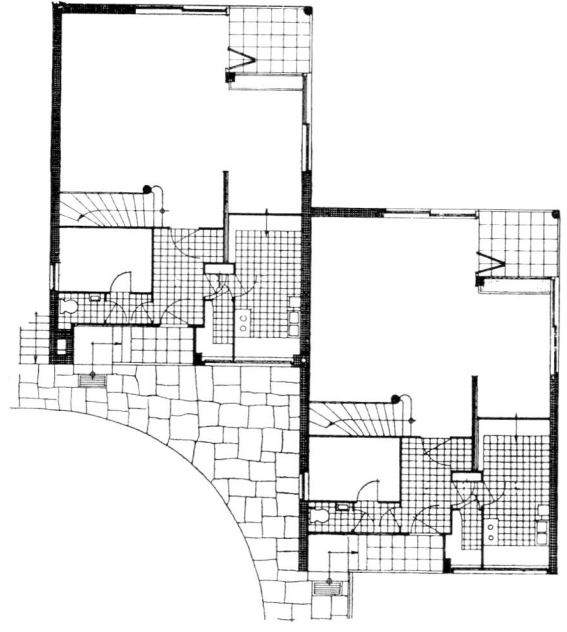

József Fischer, 1934–1935
Doppelhaus in Budapest, Ansicht;
Grundriß des ersten Stocks
Semi-detached houses in Budapest.
View. First floor plan
Maison double à Budapest, vue de
face; plan du premier étage

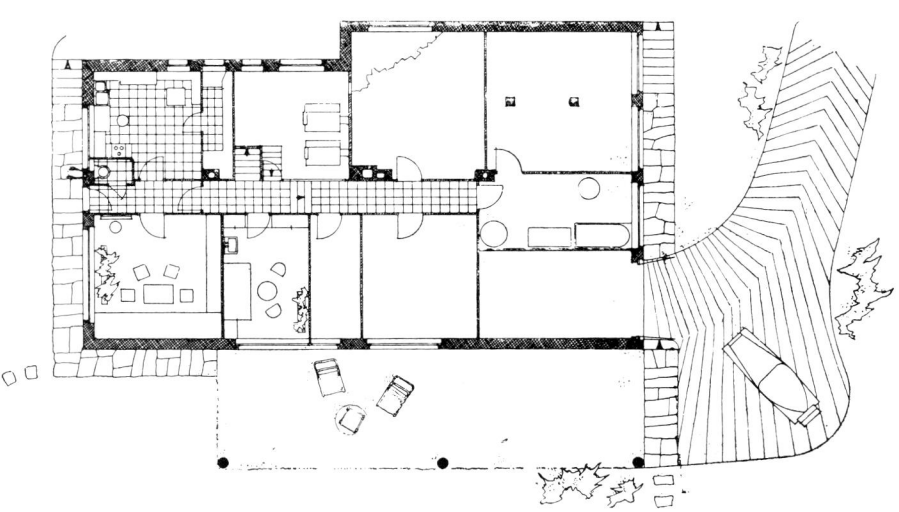

József Fischer, 1937
Villa Dr. Schild in Budapest,
Ansicht; Grundriß des Erdgeschos-
ses
House of Dr. Schild in Budapest.
View. Ground-floor plan
Villa du Dr Schild à Budapest, vue
de face; plan du rez-de-chaussée

365

Farkas Molnár, 1933
Wohnhaus in Budapest
House in Budapest
Immeuble à Budapest

József Fischer, 1936
Villa einer Opernsängerin in
Budapest
Villa belonging to an opera singer
in Budapest
Villa d'une cantatrice à Budapest

Farkas Molnár, 1932
Villa in Budapest, Westseite
Villa in Budapest. West view
Villa à Budapest, côté ouest

Farkas Molnár, 1932
Villa in Budapest, Südseite
Villa in Budapest. South view
Villa à Budapest, côté sud

UNGARN

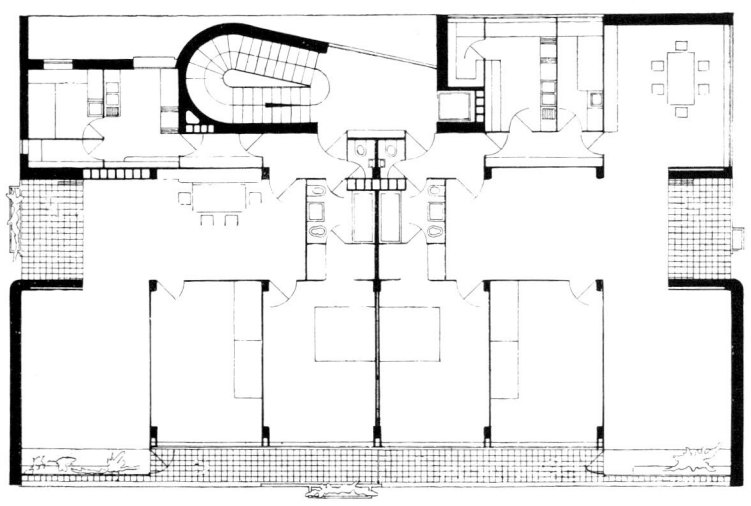

János Wanner, 1937–1938
Mietwohnhaus in Budapest,
Gartenseite; Grundriß des ersten
Stocks
Flats in Budapest. View from the
garden; first-floor plan
Immeuble à Budapest, côté jardin;
plan du premier étage

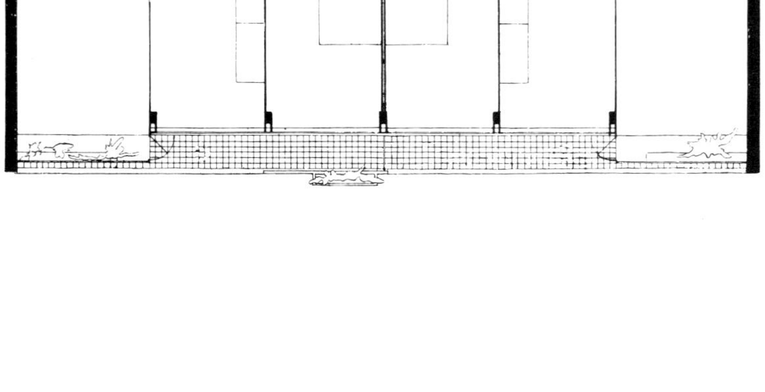

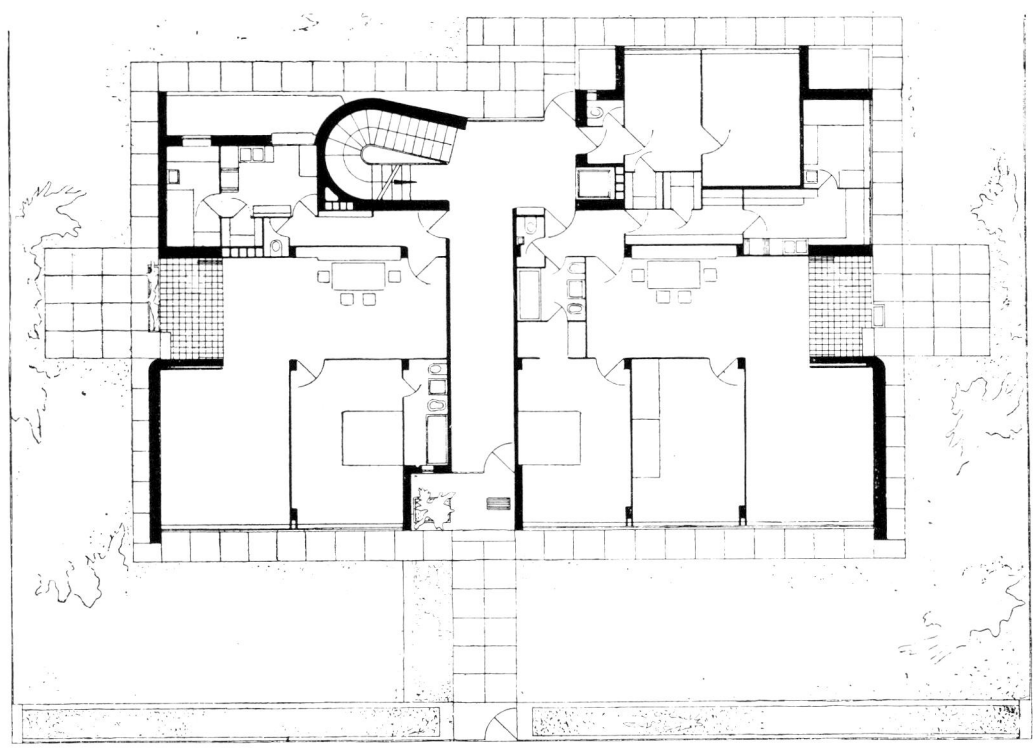

János Wanner, 1937–1938
Mietwohnhaus in Budapest,
Straßenseite; Erdgeschoßgrundriß
Villa in Budapest. View from the
road; ground-floor plan
Immeuble à Budapest, côté rue;
plan du rez-de-chaussée

Farkas Molnár und József Fischer, 1936
Heilanstalt in Pestujhely, Westfassade und Ansicht von der Straße
Nursing home in Pestujhely. West facade and view from the road
Maison de santé à Pestujhely, façade ouest et vue de la rue

Farkas Molnár, 1937
Wohnhaus in Budapest, Straßen-
seite
House in Budapest. View from the
road
Immeuble à Budapest, côté rue

**Farkas Molnár und József Fischer,
1936**
Villa in Budapest, Gartenseite
Villa in Budapest. View from the
garden
Villa à Budapest, côté jardin

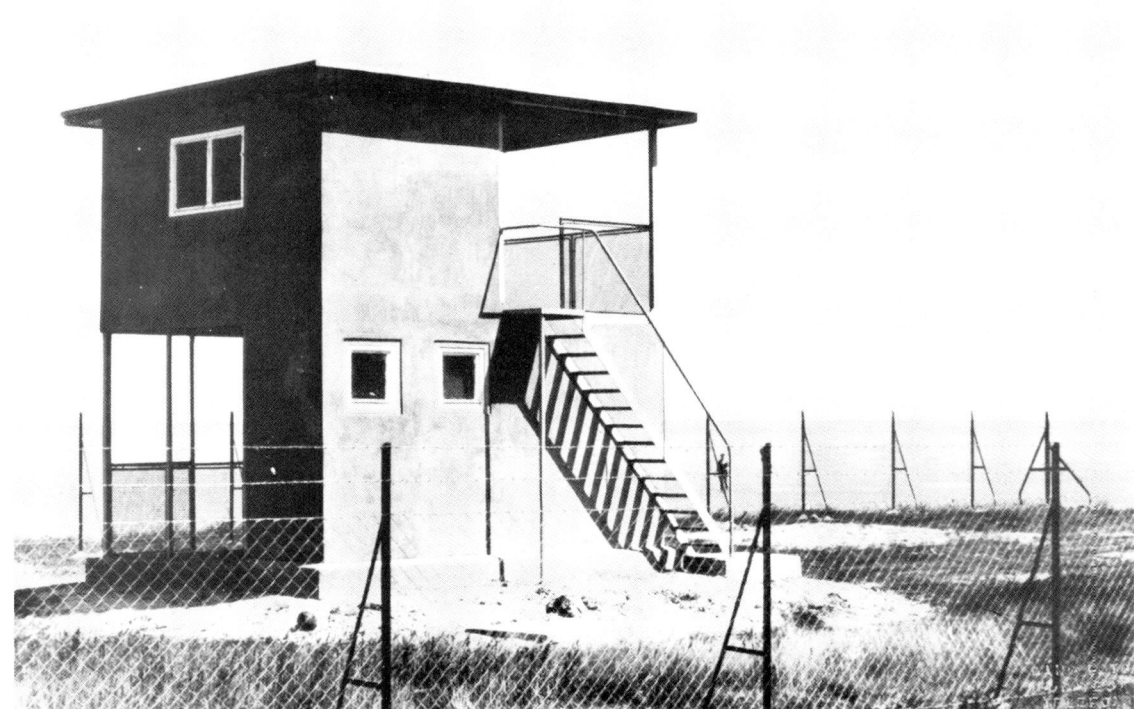

József Molnár, 1935
Einfamilienhaus in Erdliget
Detached house in Erdliget
Maison individuelle à Erdliget

József Molnár, 1931
Wochenendhaus am Plattensee
Weekend house on Lake Balaton
Maison de campagne au bord du
lac Balaton

VEREINIGTE STAATEN

George Howe und William Lescaze, 1931
Bürohochhaus der »Philadelphia Saving Fund Society« in Philadelphia, Pennsylvania
High-rise office building of the »Philadelphia Saving Fund Society« in Philadelphia, Pennsylvania
Tour de bureaux de la »Philadelphia Saving Fund Society« à Philadelphie, Pennsylvanie

George Howe und William Lescaze, 1931
Bürohochhaus der »Philadelphia Saving Fund Society« in Philadelphia, Pennsylvania
High-rise office building of the »Philadelphia Saving Fund Society« in Philadelphia, Pennsylvania
Tour de bureaux de la »Philadelphia Saving Fund Society« à Philadelphie, Pennsylvanie

George Howe und William Lescaze
Tagesschule »Oaklane« in
Philadelphia, Pennsylvania, Ansicht
von der Spielwiese; Eckfenster des
Unterrichtsraumes
»Oaklane« day school in Philadelphia Pennsylvania. View from the
play area; corner window of class-
room
Ecole »Oaklane« à Philadelphie,
Pennsylvanie, vue de la pelouse de
jeux; fenêtre d'angle de la salle de
classe

George Howe und William Lescaze, 1932
Haus F. V. Field in Connecticut
The house of F. V. Field in Connecticut
Maison F. V. Field à Connecticut

William Lescaze, 1934
Haus des Architekten in New York,
Straßenseite bei Nacht
The architect's house in New York.
View from the road by night
Maison de l'architecte à New York,
côté rue de nuit

William Lescaze
Fabrikgebäude der Kimble Glass
Co. in Vineland, New Jersey
Kimble Glass Co. factory building
in Vineland, New Jersey
Bâtiments d'usine de la Kimble
Glass Co. à Vineland, New Jersey

**William Lescaze und Earl
Heitschmidt, 1937–1938**
Gebäude der Columbia
Broadcasting System in Hollywood,
California
Columbia Broadcasting System
building in Hollywood, California
Bâtiments de la Columbia Broad-
casting System à Hollywood, Cali-
fornie

William Lescaze
Haus Curry in South Devon
The Curry house in South Devon
Maison Curry dans le Devon du Sud

William Lescaze und George Daub
Haus in Harvey Cedars, New
Jersey
House in Harvey Cedars, New
Jersey
Maison à Harvey Cedars, New Jer-
sey

Lyndon und Smith
Beecher High School in Flint, Michigan
Beecher High School in Flint, Michigan
Beecher High School à Flint, Michigan

Lyndon und Smith, 1936
Northville Grade School in
Northville, Michigan
Northville Grade School in
Northville, Michigan
Northville Grade School à North-
ville, Michigan

Richard J. Neutra, 1937
Wohnanlage in Westwood,
California, Straßenseite; Grundriß
Residential development in
Westwood, California. View from
the road. Ground Plan
Complexe d'habitation à West-
wood, Californie, côté rue; plan

Richard J. Neutra, 1936
Wohnanlage in Westwood,
California, Westseite; Nordseite
Residential development in
Westwood, California. West view.
North view
Complexe d'habitation à West-
wood, Californie, côté ouest; côte
nord

Richard J. Neutra, 1936
Wohnanlage in Westwood, California, Gesamtansicht; Grundriß
Residential development in
Westwood, California. Overall
view; ground plan
Complexe d'habitation à Westwood, Californie, vue d'ensemble;
plan

Richard J. Neutra, 1935
Villa von Josef von Sternberg in San
Fernando Valley, California; im
Vordergrund die Terrasseneinfas-
sung mit Wasserbecken
Villa of Josef von Sternberg in San
Fernando Valley, California. In the
foreground, the terrace border with
pond
Villa de Josef von Sternberg à San
Fernando Valley, Californie, au
premier plan l'encadrement de la
terrasse avec bassin

Richard J. Neutra, 1938
Villa von John Nicholas Brown auf
Fisher's Island, New Jersey,
Eingangsseite; Gartenseite
Villa of John Nicholas Brown on
Fisher's Island, New Jersey.
Entrance side; view from garden
Villa de John Nicholas Brown à
Fisher's Island, New Jersey, côté
de l'entré; côté du jardin

Richard J. Neutra, 1937
Haus Mensendieck in Palm Springs,
California
The Mensendieck house in Palm
Springs, California
Maison Mensendieck à Palm
Springs, Californie

Richard J. Neutra, 1937
Villa von Leon Barsha in North
Hollywood, California, Südseite;
Grundriß
Villa of Leon Barsha in North
Hollywood, California. South view;
ground plan
Villa de Leon Barsha à North
Hollywood, Californie, côté sud;
plan

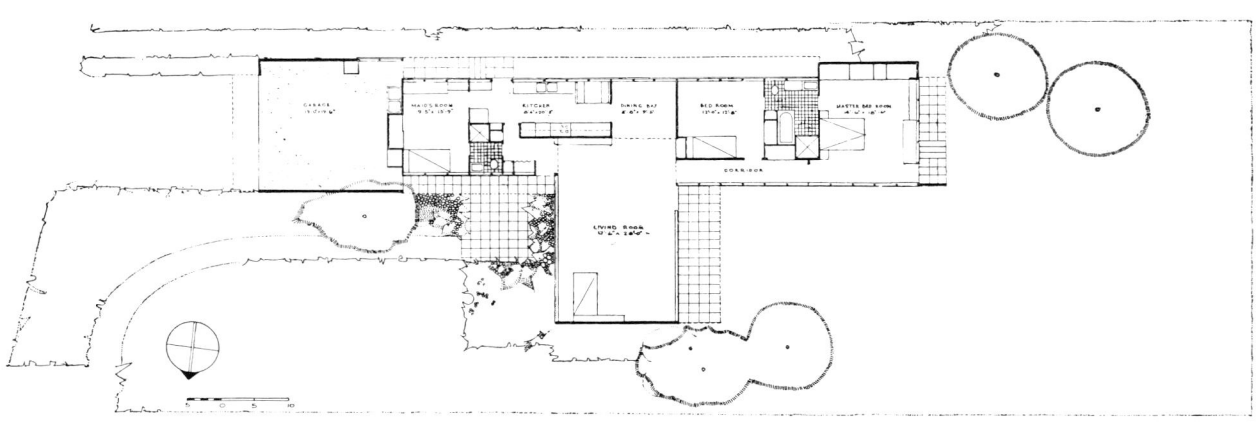

Richard J. Neutra, 1937
Villa von Edward Kaufman in
Westwood, California, Ansicht von
Südwesten; Gartenseite
Villa of Edward Kaufman in
Westwood, California. View from
the south-west and from the garden
Villa d'Edward Kaufman à West-
wood, Californie, vue du sud-ouest;
côté jardin

Albert Kahn, 1936
Fabrikgebäude der Chrysler
Corporation in Detroit, Michigan
Factory building of the Chrysler
Corporation in Detroit, Michigan
Bâtiments d'usine de la Chrysler
Corporation à Detroit, Michigan

**Jones, Roessle, Olschner und
Wiener, 1935**
Müllverbrennungsanlage in
Shreveport, Louisiana
Municipal incinerator in
Shreveport, Louisiana
Centrale d'incinération d'ordures à
Shreveport, Louisiane

**Philip L. Goodwin und Edward
Durell Stone, 1939**
The Museum of Modern Art in New
York, Straßenseite
The Museum of Modern Art in New
York. View from the road
The Museum of Modern Art à New
York, côté rue

**Smith-Miller, Sanders und Breck,
1939**
Chilenischer Pavillon auf der Weltausstellung in New York
Chilean pavilion at the World Fair
in New York
Pavillon chilien à l'Exposition Universelle de New York

**Louis Skidmore, Nathaniel Owings
und John Moss, 1939**
Pavillon Venezuelas auf der Welt-
ausstellung in New York
Venezuelan pavilion at the World
Fair in New York
Pavillon vénézuélien à l'Exposition
Universelle de New York

**Lucio Costa und Oscar Niemeyer
Soares, 1939**
Brasilianischer Pavillon auf der
Weltausstellung in New York
Brazilian pavilion at the World Fair
in New York
Pavillon brésilien à l'Exposition
Universelle de New York

Michael Scott, 1939
Pavillon Irlands auf der Weltaus-
stellung in New York
Irish pavilion at the World Fair in
New York
Pavillon irlandais à l'Exposition
Universelle de New York

Die Abbildungen wurden folgenden Publikationen entnommen:

Richard Döcker, Terrassentyp, Stuttgart 1929

Glass in Modern Construction. Its Place in Architectural Design and Decoration, New York und London 1937

Arthur Korn, Glas im Bau und als Gebrauchsgegenstand, Berlin o.J.

Alberto Sartoris, Gli Elementi dell'Architettura Funzionale. Sintesi panoramica dell'Architettura Moderna. Terza Edizione, Mailand 1941

Baukunst, 5. Jhrgg. 1929

Der Baumeister. Monatshefte für Architektur und Baupraxis, 27. Jhrgg. 1929; 29. Jhrgg. 1931; 30. Jhrgg. 1932

Innendekoration. Die gesamte Wohnungskunst in Bild und Wort, 42. Jhrgg. 1931; 43. Jhrgg. 1932; 45. Jhrgg. 1934; 47. Jhrgg. 1936

Moderne Bauformen. Monatshefte für Architektur und Raumkunst, 29. Jhrgg. 1930

Wasmuths Monatshefte für Baukunst & Städtebau, 11. Jhrgg. 1927; 13. Jhrgg. 1929; 14. Jhrgg. 1930; 15. Jhrgg. 1931